The Old Testament

Amy-Jill Levine, Ph.D.

PUBLISHED BY:

THE GREAT COURSES
Corporate Headquarters
4840 Westfields Boulevard, Suite 500
Chantilly, Virginia 20151-2299
Phone: 1-800-832-2412
Fax: 703-378-3819
www.thegreatcourses.com

Copyright © The Teaching Company, 2001

Printed in the United States of America

This book is in copyright. All rights reserved.

Without limiting the rights under copyright reserved above,
no part of this publication may be reproduced, stored in
or introduced into a retrieval system, or transmitted,
in any form, or by any means
(electronic, mechanical, photocopying, recording, or otherwise),
without the prior written permission of
The Teaching Company.

Amy-Jill Levine, Ph.D.
E. Rhodes and Leona B. Carpenter Professor
Vanderbilt University Divinity School/
Graduate Department of Religion

Professor Amy-Jill Levine earned her B.A. with high honors in English and Religion at Smith College, where she graduated *magna cum laude* and was a member of Phi Beta Kappa. Her M.A. and Ph.D. in Religion are from Duke University, where she was a Gurney Harris Kearns Fellow and held the W. D. Davies Instructorship in Biblical Studies. Before moving to Vanderbilt, she was Sara Lawrence Lightfoot Associate Professor and chair of the Department of Religion at Swarthmore College.

Professor Levine's numerous books, articles, and essays address such topics as Second-Temple Judaism, Christian origins, and biblical women's roles and representations; she has written commentaries on Ruth, Esther, and Daniel, as well as on the Gospels of Matthew and Mark. She is currently completing a manuscript for Harvard University Press on Jewish narratives from the Hellenistic period and a major commentary on the Book of Esther for Walter de Gruyter Press (Berlin). Professor Levine has served on the editorial boards of the *Journal of Biblical Literature* and the *Catholic Biblical Quarterly*, among other publications, and has held office in the Society of Biblical Literature and the Association for Jewish Studies. Among her awards are grants from the Mellon Foundation, the National Endowment for the Humanities, and the American Council of Learned Societies.

A widely sought speaker, Levine has given lectures and workshops throughout the United States and Canada for universities, biblical associations, synagogues, temples, churches, and interfaith and civic groups, as well as two series of lectures at Chautauqua in the Hall of Philosophy.

As a graduate student at Duke, Levine was initially prevented from teaching New Testament in the Divinity School by an administrator who did not think it appropriate that a Jew would teach this material. "You can teach Old Testament," he told her. "I don't do Old Testament," she said; "You do now," was his response. Thus began her ever-growing fascination with the subject of these lectures. Within a semester, the administrator was no longer at Duke and Levine's teaching opportunities broadened, but she chose to continue in the Old Testament classroom while adding courses in the New Testament. Completing coursework in both Old Testament/*Tanakh* and Christian origins, Levine has been studying and teaching both topics ever since.

Levine and her husband, Jay Geller, Ph.D. (who also teaches religion at Vanderbilt), live with their children, Sarah Elizabeth and Alexander David, in Nashville, Tennessee. ■

Table of Contents

INTRODUCTION

Professor Biography i
Course Scope 1

LECTURE GUIDES

LECTURE 1
In the Beginning 3

LECTURE 2
Adam and Eve 7

LECTURE 3
Murder, Flood, Dispersion 13

LECTURE 4
Abraham, Sarah, and Hagar 18

LECTURE 5
Isaac 23

LECTURE 6
The Jacob Saga 27

LECTURE 7
Folklore Analysis and Type Scenes 31

LECTURE 8
Moses and Exodus 36

LECTURE 9
The God of Israel 41

LECTURE 10
Covenant and Law, Part I 46

Table of Contents

LECTURE 11
Covenant and Law, Part II 51

LECTURE 12
The "Conquest" 57

LECTURE 13
The Book of Judges, Part I 62

LECTURE 14
The Book of Judges, Part II 68

LECTURE 15
Samuel and Saul 74

LECTURE 16
King David 79

LECTURE 17
From King Solomon to Preclassical Prophecy 83

LECTURE 18
The Prophets and the Fall of the North 88

LECTURE 19
The Southern Kingdom 92

LECTURE 20
Babylonian Exile 96

LECTURE 21
Restoration and Theocracy 100

LECTURE 22
Wisdom Literature 104

LECTURE 23
Life in the Diaspora 108

Table of Contents

LECTURE 24
Apocalyptic Literature 114

SUPPLEMENTAL MATERIAL

Timeline 117
Glossary 120
Bibliography 133

The Old Testament

Scope:

The Bible has been labeled, correctly, as the foundation document of Western thought. It is read in synagogues, temples, and churches; it is cited on the floor of the Senate and from the bench in the courtroom. Contemporary politics is inextricably intertwined with it, from conflict in the Middle East to the claim by many in the United States that a return to "biblical values" is warranted. The Bible influenced the Pilgrims to leave England in the 17th century; it inspired the founders of the new republic in the eighteenth; it roused both slave and abolitionist to seek a new Moses and sponsor a new Exodus in the nineteenth and the Jews to establish a homeland in the twentieth. Missionaries, with Bible in hand, journeyed to Asia, Africa, and South America, and among the indigenous populations they met, the Bible galvanized attempts to throw off the yoke of colonialism. Its influence permeates Western literature, from medieval plays to modern novels, art, music, theatre, film and dance; its prophetic calls for social justice challenge all readers to reevaluate their own behavior even as its Wisdom literature challenges our views of God. Replete with genres ranging from myth and saga to law and proverb, containing dry political history and erotic love poetry, informed by a world view much different than our own, these texts are a compendium of a people's sacred story. And that story is the foundation document of Judaism and the first part of the canon of the church.

These twenty-four lectures offer an introduction to the history, literature, and religion of ancient Israel and early Judaism as it is presented in the collection of texts called the Old Testament, the Hebrew Bible, and the *Tanakh*. Not all books will, or even could, be covered; the content of certain books, such as Genesis, could easily fill twenty-four lectures alone, as could the stories of certain figures, such as the Patriarchs and Matriarchs, Moses, and David. Attention is given not only to the content of the biblical books but also to the debates over their meaning and the critical methods through which they have been interpreted. Often, a book will be examined by means of an analysis of a representative text or figure in it.

The lectures presuppose only a very general familiarity with the Bible's major figures and themes (e.g., Adam and Eve, Moses, the Ten Commandments, David and Bathsheba); biblical literacy, as sociologists have noted, is on the wane in the West. Although students do not need to follow the lectures with an open Bible, reading the texts listed at the top of each of the outlines will enhance appreciation for the material.

Oriented toward historical context and literary import, the lectures do not avoid raising issues of religious concern. The goal of an academic course in biblical studies should not be to undermine religious faith. Rather, it should provide members of faith communities with richer insights into the literature that forms their bedrock. Even were one to argue that the text is divinely inspired or dictated by God, one might still want to know as much as possible about the particulars: Why these words? Why this order? Why this social context? Why this translation? ∎

N.B. Many scriptural quotations in the lectures are translated by Dr. Levine directly from the Hebrew and thus may vary slightly with the text of standard printed editions in English. In other cases she draws from the New Revised Standard Version (NRSV), the King James Version (KJV) and the New English Bible (NEB).

In the Beginning
(Genesis 1)
Lecture 1

By the very fact we've got two different definitions and two different communities of faith, already we can see that there are a variety of matters that we can express, controversial issues, method of approach.

This opening lecture introduces not only the content of the Old Testament/*Tanakh* but also a number of issues—historical, theological, and aesthetic—involved in its interpretation. Following a brief description of biblical materials and the means by which they may be appreciated, we turn to several critical tools that are useful for gaining a deeper appreciation of Scripture and some of the technical terms used in its academic study. The general discussion concludes by noting a few biblical contributions to Western culture. At last entering the text, we begin "in the beginning," with the first chapter of Genesis, examining test cases for the diversity of interpretive approaches.

The biblical story spans time from creation (Gen. 1) to Judaism's encounter with Hellenism in the wake of Alexander the Great (Daniel), and for each setting, it provides a variety of literatures. Its genres include cosmological myths and stories of origin (Gen. 1–11), sagas of culture heroes (Gen. 12–50, Joshua, Judges), law codes (Leviticus, Deuteronomy), prophetic oracles (Amos, Isaiah), court tales (Esther, Dan. 1–6), and apocalyptic visions (Zech. 9–14, Dan. 7–12). Among its authors are storytellers, bureaucrats, prophets, priests, scribes, and visionaries; and it's subjects address such diverse questions as: Who are we? What is our history? What are our standards of morality? How do we relate to those outside our community? How, and whom, shall we worship?

This diversity of genres, authors, audiences, and issues requires a complex approach for achieving a well-rounded cognizance. Greater understanding of the corpus requires recognition that it is an anthology, with texts written in different times and locations to meet different concerns. A deeper familiarity comes with knowledge of the ancient Near East and the understanding that what was normative then—such as animal sacrifice and a geocentric universe—is normative no longer. Appreciation of the biblical story is enhanced by a familiarity with how individual materials fit together, chapter by chapter, book by book. Because the Bible is a foundation document not only for Judaism and Christianity but also for much contemporary culture, we do not come to it untouched. Knowledge of materials adapted by communities of faith, children's books and movies, artists and politicians facilitates consideration of how such adaptations affect our own interpretations. Study provides an opportunity to test not only our assumptions but also our biblically based values. The wider the number of critical tools we use and the consequent range of questions we pose, the more complete our appreciation will be.

Religious considerations inevitably enter biblical discussions. An academic approach to Scripture should be sensitive to religious commitments but neither presuppose them, nor proselytize for them. It should enhance rather than threaten faith; any consideration of the text as divinely inspired should include appreciation for the times, places, and peoples wherein and to whom the inspiration occurred. The academic approach should give believers, agnostics, atheists, and those whose religions fall outside the biblical purview all a deeper understanding of the text.

Among the methods used in the academic study of the Bible, the following have had a substantial impact. Historical-critical approaches seek to situate biblical material in its original context and test the accuracy of its presentation. Archaeology has been used to prove, disprove, and understand biblical content and philological investigation of the language of the text—primarily Hebrew, with some in the cognate, Aramaic—makes translation more precise. There can also be a literary-critical approach, revealing textual artistry and complexity. Recognition of literary conventions ("type scenes"); tracing of themes throughout several narratives; and attention to irony, puns, and multiple interpretations of the same passage increase appreciation of the narrative. Even those who believe that a text recounts a historical event or that "history" is the only approach worth pursing might still consider the manner in which the event is recounted: How is the story told? With what agenda? For whose benefit?

Like most disciplines, biblical studies has its own technical terminology. To make the discipline less parochial, scholars have developed alternative designations for dates and texts. B.C. ("Before Christ") and A.D. (Latin: "in the year of our Lord") often become B.C.E. ("Before the Common Era") and C.E. ("Common Era"). "Old Testament" is a Christian designation; Jews refer to the "Tanakh" an acronym for Torah (Pentateuch), Nevi'im (Prophets), and Ketuvim (Writings). Secular classrooms increasingly use the (ostensibly) neutral "Hebrew Scriptures." I shall often use the generic "Bible."

To make referencing convenient, manuscripts were divided, in the early Middle Ages, into chapters and verses that remain in use. Chapter numbers follow the name of the book: Gen. 12 means the twelfth chapter of the book of Genesis. When the chapter number is followed by a colon or period and another number, the reference is to a verse: Gen. 1:1 is the first verse of chapter 1. Verse and chapter divisions are a convenience, but they should not guide analysis. Other terms will be introduced throughout the course; a glossary also appears in the back of this book.

Although these lectures do not presuppose extensive familiarity with biblical content, they do presume some general awareness, for example, of such figures as Adam and Moses. Literature is replete with biblical references; consider Steinbeck's *East of Eden*; Toni Morrison's *Song of Solomon*; Faulkner's *Absalom, Absalom!*; Archibald MacLeish's *J. B.*; and so on. Much art, literature, film, and dance adapt or refer to biblical subjects.

We will also look at cross-cultural comparisons. "In the beginning" (better: "when, in the beginning") is perhaps a response to the foundation myth of the Babylonian Empire, the *Enumah Elish*, which begins, "when on high …" In the *Enumah Elisha*, Apsu (fresh water) and Tiamat (salt water) are male and female gods of chaos. Genesis depicts the uncreated as impersonal (*Tohu wavohu*—"without form and void"). Marduk, Babylon's tutelary deity, assisted by seven wind gods, inflates Tiamat with air, kills her, and creates earth and the sky from her divided carcass. In Genesis, the divine "spirit" or "wind" hovers over the "deep" (Heb: Tehom) before dividing the waters. From the blood of a dead god, Marduk creates humanity to be slaves of the gods. Genesis gives humankind a divine component, "Let us make the human being in our image ..." and enjoins responsible power rather than slavery: "let them have dominion over ..." (1:16).

Genesis 1 portrays a universal, singular, omnipotent Deity who creates by word (but see Gen. 2). The Deity is singular but speaks with the "plural of majesty" or "royal 'we.'" The Deity is never described and cannot be imaged, but humanity is in the likeness of the divine. ∎

Suggested Reading

Note: The bibliography at the back of this book lists the major series containing commentaries on all biblical books, standard academic encyclopedias and dictionaries, and individual volumes.

James L. Kugel, *Traditions of the Bible: A Guide to the Bible as It Was at the Start of the Common Era.*

Susan Niditch, *Ancient Israelite Religion.*

John Rogerson and Philip Davies, *The Old Testament World.*

Questions to Consider

1. Cultural critics have claimed that biblical literacy is on the decline among today's youth. Is the text as important, culturally or religiously, today as it has been in the past?

2. Given the Bible's role in religious communities, should its study be different than, for example, that of ancient Greek literature or any other subject area?

3. The Bible took shape in antiquity, in the cultural climates of Sumer, Assyria, Canaan, Babylon, Persia, and so on. Given that that world is not our world, how do we bridge the gap to achieve understanding?

Adam and Eve
(Genesis 2:4b–3:28)
Lecture 2

> The Garden of Eden is the perfect garden. You're supposed to work it; you're supposed to till it. But the ground yields its fruit. There's no struggle. There's only joy. It's work, but the best sort of work possible.

The Garden of Eden, like the rest of primeval history (Genesis 1–11) is "myth," a foundational story that undergirds cultural norms and explains communal identity. Many scholars suggest that Genesis 2–3, the "J" cosmogony (it uses the name "YHWH" [German: JHWH, the "Y"= the German "J"] for "Lord,"), was composed during Solomon's reign (c. 900 B.C.E.). Three hundred to four hundred years later, the P (Priestly) writer placed Genesis 1 before the J account, creating a new lens by which Eden may be understood. This lecture follows Gen. 2–3, selectively, episode by episode, to highlight its complexity, the effects of Genesis 1 on its interpretation, its possible ancient Near Eastern connections, and the questions that remain debated.

In the beginning: What to notice? What to ask? The first words spoken, "let there be light," mark the first day, but sun and moon ("greater" and "lesser lights") appear on the fourth. Readers unfamiliar with biblical law frequently consider the Bible as a series of "Thou shalt nots"; the first commandment is, however, a positive one: "Be fruitful ..." Genesis 1 offers one explanation for the Sabbath, the divine rest (cf. Exod. 20:8–11); Deut. 5:15 inscribes another, that is, release from Egyptian slavery, into the Decalogue.

The Priestly writers (more on them later) composed Gen. 1:1–2:4a as an introduction to the earlier story of the Garden of Eden, Adam, Eve, and the snake (Gen. 2–3). For some readers, this juxtaposition creates contradictions, and for others it does not. Whereas Gen. 1 depicts a simultaneous creation, *ex nihilo*, of "male and female," Gen. 2 presents a fashioned, sexually indeterminate being. Gen. 2:7, "Then the Lord God formed man from the dust from the ground ..." reflects a Hebrew pun: "Man" is *ha-adam*, "the adam"; "adam" derives from *adamah*—arable soil or, here, "ground." Better translations would speak of an "earthling from the dust of the earth" or a "human" from the "humus," the loamy soil. The juxtaposed Gen. 1 may be seen to ensure a view of divine power and transcendence. The "earthling" is then planted in the Garden of Eden to "till it and keep it" (2:15). Life in Eden (the name means "pleasure") is one of easy work; it is not, however, "dominion over the earth." The agricultural paradise perhaps reflects the dreams of subsistence farmers or, perhaps, the romantic view of Jerusalem's court for the countryside.

God informs the human, "Of the tree of the knowledge of good and evil you shall not eat, for in the day you eat from it you will surely die" (colloquially: "you'll drop dead" [2:17]). This verse prompts theological questions, Is God tempting the human? Does the Deity know what will happen? Has the Deity planned the "fall"? Was humanity originally mortal or immortal? The tree recollects other myths of forbidden fruits and sacred trees (e.g., Ygdrassil, Jason's tree on which the golden fleece hangs). The specific ways each culture tells its story, then, permits understanding of that culture's values.

God next observes: "It is not good that the earthling should be alone. I will make him an *ezer k'negdo*," "a helper as his partner" (NRSV) or, traditionally, "a helper fit for him" (2:18). Is this "helper" to be equal or a subordinate? The idiom "fit for" indicates something corresponding, appropriate, suitable: *ha-adam* requires someone "like" him. The Hebrew *Ezer*, help or helper, is often a predicate of the Deity. Instead of next creating woman, "out of the ground the Lord God formed every animal of the field and every bird of the air, and brought them to the human to see what it would call them." Adam names the animals but finds no "partner fit for him." What then does the woman do to help? Is she needed to challenge man to reach his potential, to encourage him, or even act for him (as, for example, Rebecca does for Jacob or Bathsheba for the dying David)? Or is the answer more utilitarian: only women can "help" men propagate? Does Genesis 1, "Be fruitful and multiply," lead us to this interpretation? This scene, compared to Gen. 1:26–27, prompted the early Medieval Jewish myth of Lilith, the first woman, who rebelled against God and Adam.

Woman's creation from man's "side" or "rib" stimulates cross-cultural and anthropological observations. Genesis may have been influenced by, or serve as a response to, the Sumerian Dilmun (paradise) myth. This myth recounts how the god Enki is cursed by the goddess Ninhursag, because he ate plants she bore painlessly. Ninhursag then creates the goddess Nin-Ti, "lady of the rib" or "lady who makes live," to heal his broken body. Adam may be seen as "giving birth" to Eve, as Dionysius is born from Zeus's "thigh" and Athena, from his head. Some anthropologists suggest that such stories show a co-optation of women's biology: Although Adam's parturition is clean and painless, women can recreate the event only in a messy, painful manner. The rib has also been read as promoting gender equality. One Midrash (rabbinic story) states that woman was not taken from man's head, lest she lord it over him, nor his feet, lest he walk all over her. She is from his side, and they are partners.

Contrary to popular belief, it is not woman who tempts man, but the snake and the tree itself that tempt woman. God had forbidden the earthling merely to eat from the tree. In her response to the snake, the woman adds: "But God said, 'Neither shall you touch it, lest you die.'" According to Phyllis Trible, this comment makes Eve both a "theologian and a translator." According to one popular conservative biblical commentary: "Sin begins with some distortion of the truth." We might also wonder who told the woman about the tree: the Deity? The man?

The conversation and what happens subsequently are often misconstrued. First, the serpent speaks accurately: "You will not die, for God knows that when you eat of it your eyes will be opened, and you will be like the gods, knowing good and evil." Second, the woman's decision is thoughtful: "When the woman saw that the tree was good for food, and that it was a delight to the eyes, and that the tree was to be desired to make one wise, she took of its fruit and she ate." And third, she does not tempt man: "She also gave some to her husband [or new "man"] and he ate."

The Temptation's numerous interpretations include the following. Socially, the temptation may be read as a warning to men against allowing their wives to speak with a stranger, the proverbial "snake in the grass." Historically,

Adam and Eve driven out of paradise.

it may indicate the dangerous power of women in the royal harem, such as those who tempted Solomon with their foreign practices (1 Kgs. 11). Some forms of gnosticism, an early common-era religious movement, suggested that the woman brings *Gnosis* ("knowledge") to a world kept ignorant by a foolish god. And from the New Testament, 1 Tim. 2:14 reads, "Adam was not deceived, but the woman was deceived and became a transgressor." That is, Adam was not seduced; his choice was one of conscious solidarity with his partner.

As a result of the transgression, the couple experiences not death, but loss of innocence or shame, and this loss is compounded by punishments ("curse" is not used). Most translations render 3:16: "I will greatly multiply your pain in childbearing; in pain you shall give birth to children." Carol Meyers translates instead: "I will greatly increase your work and your pregnancies; along with work you shall give birth to children." The term for "work" is the same used in 3:17d: "In work you shall eat of it all the days of your life." The term translated "childbearing" means "pregnancies." Women's lot is thus to work in two spheres: procreation and production. "Yet your desire shall be for your man [husband] and he shall rule over you" (3:16c). Although the "rule" (*mashal*), is not tyrannical (it is associated with "good kings," such as Solomon and Hezekiah, cf. 1 Kgs. 4:3), it does mean "have dominion over" (cf. Gen. 1:18). "Rule" may also suggest "prevail," as in "be the primary economic support." Does the myth tell women that sexual desire is "natural" even though they may die in childbirth (as does Rachel)?

The man's punishment is prefaced by a rationale that is missing from the other two: "Because you have listened to the voice of your wife ..." The phrase is recollected in the expulsion of Hagar and Ishmael (Gen. 21:12). It also responds to Adam's complaint (3:8): "*The woman whom you gave to be with me*, she gave me the fruit and I ate."

Having become like gods, knowing good and evil, man and woman must leave Eden. And so we come to Cain, the flood, Babel. Given this trajectory, the election of Abraham indicates the final attempt at universal stability. ∎

Suggested Reading

Gary Anderson, Michael Stone, and Johannes Tromp (eds.), *Literature on Adam and Eve: Collected Essays*, Studies in Veteris Testamenti Pseudepigrapa.

James Barr, *The Garden of Eden and the Hope of Immortality*.

Kristen Kvam, Linda S. Schearing, and Valarie H. Ziegler, *Eve and Adam: Jewish, Christian and Muslim Readings on Genesis and Gender*.

Carol Meyers, *Discovering Eve: Ancient Israelite Women in Context*.

Questions to Consider

1. This story of Eden is never mentioned again in the Old Testament/*Tanakh* (its next canonical appearances are the Old Testament Apocrypha/Deuterocanonical writings). How then, if at all, does the story affect interpretations of later texts (e.g., the man speaks of leaving home to cleave to his wife; do most male characters do this)?

2. How closely do later retellings (Milton's *Paradise Lost*, the film *The Bible*, popular cultural renditions) adhere to the text?

3. Is Eden a desirable place? A return to childhood? A prison?

Murder, Flood, Dispersion
(Genesis 4:1–11:32)
Lecture 3

God goes with Adam and Eve when they leave Eden. Eve has a child, Cain; it looks like things are going to be okay. But it turns out, as we go through the rest of the primeval history from Genesis 4 through Genesis 11, things get worse and worse. ... We have humankind becoming so cruel, so awful that God decides to wipe out creation with a flood.

Genesis 1–11 depicts the increasing alienation of humanity from one another, the uneasy relationship between animal husbandry and agriculture, the wilderness and the city-state, and the increasing alienation between humanity and God. This lecture investigates these themes through analysis of the stories of Cain and Abel, Noah's flood, and the Tower of Babel. The lecture also observes the tantalizing hints in the primeval history of other myths, likely known to the Bible's early audiences but now lost to history.

The story of Cain and Abel continues the downward spiral of history begun with the expulsion from Eden. Genesis 4 may recreate Israel's early struggles between agriculture and animal husbandry. The account may favor animal sacrifices over harvest offerings. Supporting this view is its insistence on the potency of blood. Was Abel's sacrifice more fitting because he brings "of the *firstlings* of his flock and of their *fat portions*" while Cain brings just "An offering of the fruit of the ground" (4:3–4)? Cain, the founder of the first city and, therefore, of sustainable agricultural produce, prevails, but his pastoral brother remains (nostalgically?) mourned. The notion of primogeniture, followed here, is contradicted by later biblical stories. In the Old Testament/*Tanakh*, birth order is less important than one's merit and divine sponsorship.

Some historians propose that Cain's story is an etiology for the *Kenites*, a group represented by Moses's in-laws (Jdg. 1:16) and, likely, Jael, the tent-peg–wielding heroine of Deborah's Song (Jdg. 4–5). They worship YHWH and settle in Canaan (1 Sam. 30:29) but are not members of Israel. The mark of "Cain" (a cognate to "Kenite") may represent a tribal insignia. The connection may reveal Israel's uneasiness with these neighbors.

The absence of explicit rationale for God's rejection of Cain's sacrifice has also prompted more theological interpretations. One murder equals the death of one-quarter of the world's population. Sacrifice cannot buy divine favor.

Along with the ever-popular queries concerning Cain's wife, in which the Bible displays no interest, the primeval history hints at more complete mythic antecedents. " … all the days of Enoch were 365 years. And Enoch walked with God; and he was not, for God took him" (Gen. 5:21–24). Because Enoch does not appear to have died, messianic speculation will attach to him in the Second Temple period. Enoch may symbolize the sanctity of time; 365 is not an arbitrary number. The Babylonian myths also record that the seventh antediluvian hero was taken by the gods (to be a servant).

Mythic speculation attaches to the *Nephilim*, the "fallen ones," who "were on the earth in those days … when the sons of God came into the daughters of men, and they bore children to them. These were the mighty men of old … giants in the earth" (6:1-4). The relation to the "daughters of men" prompts associations with both ancient Near Eastern and, especially, Greek myths (e.g., Europa, Io, Semele). Num. 13:33 counts among the Canaanite population Nephilim; that Joshua conquers them highlights Israel's ability. Perhaps the Nephilim represent the royal court: the "sons of God" (cf. 2 Sam. 7). Did they seduce women they should have protected (e.g., David and Bathsheba; Amnon and Tamar [2 Sam. 11–13]); did they rebel against God's representative (e.g., Absalom's civil war [2 Sam. 13–20])? Does the story argue against intermarriage, perhaps reflecting the breakdown of the generation of the "sons of God," such as Solomon?

This situation leads to the story of Noah, which is by no means a children's story. Problems begin with Noah's characterization. He is "a righteous man, blameless in his generation; Noah walked with God" (6:9). But the comparison to his generation is hardly complimentary. Nor does Noah, unlike

Abraham for Sodom, Moses for Israel, and several of his counterparts in ancient Near Eastern flood stories, advocate for humanity. Noah's is only one of a flood of ancient Near Eastern and Greek deluge tales; other flood heroes include Atrahasis, Zuisudra, Deucalion and Pyrrha, and—from Tablet XI of the Gilgamesh epic—Utnapishtim. Comparisons between Utnapishtim and Noah indicate a shared mythic structure. Both heroes, warned by gods about the flood, build boats. Utnapishtim's is a cube, but the design is in both cases divinely given. Neither boat seems to have a rudder. Both survive a flood caused by rain descending from the vault of the heavens and subterranean waters coming up (the cosmology promoted by Gen. 1). The earth is being un-created and dissolving into watery chaos. Both arrive on a mountain and offer sacrifices. In the Gilgamesh epic, the gods "Smelled the savor, smelled the sweet savor; the gods crowded like flies about the sacrificer." Gen. 8:21 reads: "When YHWH smelled the pleasing odor, he said in his heart: 'I will never again curse the ground … '"

The comparison also aids in determining cultural values. Informed by the gods/God of the flood, Utnapishtim weeps; Noah does nothing. Unlike Utnapishtim, he is mortal, flawed, and not to be considered divine. Utnapishtim is secretly warned by the god Ea; the gods find humankind too noisy and, therefore, intend destruction. Instructed by Ea to lie about his ark, Utnapishtim tells his neighbors he is attempting to escape from the threats of the god Enlil; ironically, they help him build. The Genesis God regrets the evil—not the noise—of humankind; there is no secrecy, warning, or demand for repentance: humanity's fate is sealed. Utnapishtim takes on board craftspeople; Noah brings only his immediate family. For the primeval history, "culture" is an ambivalent category (e.g., Cain's descendant, the violent Lamech, is the progenitor of musicians and metal workers [Gen. 4:17–24]). Although Utnapishtim attempts to convince Gilgamesh that immortality can never again be achieved, Gilgamesh nevertheless obtains the flower of immortality at the bottom of the sea (i.e., he personally experiences a flood). Falling asleep on reaching land, he awakes to discover a snake has taken the flower. For Genesis, there is no longer the possibility of immortality, of the human becoming divine. Genesis emphasizes justice (the elimination of evil) and mercy, as God establishes a covenant with "as many as came out of the ark" (9:8).

The Noachide Covenant extends, likely through editing by the Priestly (P) writers, motifs from earlier chapters. The sign of the "bow"—a weapon of war—signals peace, just as the mark on Cain signals protection. Other such signs include, notably, circumcision. Gen. 9:1ff. repeat 1:28: "Be fruitful and multiply and fill the earth." Noah and his family receive new dietary regulations: "As I gave you the green plants [the language resembles Gen. 1:29], I give you everything" (9:3); humanity is no longer vegetarian. But, echoing Gen. 1:26–27 and Abel's murder: they "shall not eat flesh with its life, that is, its blood ... whoever sheds the blood of man, by man shall his blood be shed; for God made man in his own image." The notice in Gen. 7:2–3 that the animals boarded seven by seven rather than two by two (Gen. 6:19; 7:9) not only ensures animals for Noah's sacrifice but also anticipates the categories of clean and unclean foods detailed in Lev. 11.

Just as the forbidden fruit brings knowledge as well as shame, so does Noah's viniculture comfort even as it leads to drunkenness. Noah is introduced with the prophecy "Out of the ground which YHWH has cursed, this one shall bring us relief from our work and from the toil of our hands" (Gen. 5:29). That Noah is the first person whose birth is recorded after Adam's death makes this prediction poignant. Noah "drank the wine, and became drunk, and lay uncovered in his tent." Fruit leads him back to the Edenic, but now inappropriate, nakedness.

What happens next is indeterminate; an earlier story appears to have been suppressed. We are told that Ham saw his father uncovered and informed his brothers Shem and Japhet; the brothers, walking backward in order not to witness Noah's shame, cover him. "When Noah awoke from his wine and knew what his youngest son had done to him, he said 'Cursed be Canaan'" (Gen. 9:25). What was "done"? Why curse Canaan? Cross-cultural parallel suggests the something "done" was castration. This is a common mythic motif describing the transfer of powers from father (gods) to sons. ■

Suggested Reading

Lloyd R. Bailey, *Noah: The Person and the Story in History and Tradition*.

Alan Dundes (ed.), *The Flood Myth*.

Questions to Consider

1. What are today's equivalents for "sacrifice"—a practice in antiquity as common as we find watching television?

2. Is Noah a hero? Is his story comforting or threatening? Why would ancient Israel so describe its flood story's protagonist and its God?

3. Why does Israel detail, at the beginning of its sacred history, God's disappointments and humanity's continual failures?

Abraham, Sarah, and Hagar
(Genesis 11:26–21:34)
Lecture 4

> The primeval history is a story of humankind's increasing alienation from God, from each other, and from the land. ... This is the story of the Tower of Babel, in which humankind unites altogether on the plain of Shinar—that is by the way Babylon—in order to build a giant tower to get up to God.

The tower of Babel (Gen. 11) is humanity's final, united fall. Re-creation with Noah proves a failure, and God will have to start again. Babel may polemicize against Solomon's overextended economy and international labor force. It may parody the Babylonian *ziqqurats*, thought to be bridges between heaven and earth. Such bridges are not built through independent human initiative; they require divine partnership, as the next several lectures on the "patriarchal sagas" (Genesis 12–50) reveal.

The stories of the Patriarchs (Abraham, Isaac, and Jacob) appear to be set in the late Bronze Age, c. 1750 B.C.E., although the accounts were written centuries later, as evidenced by obvious anachronisms (e.g., references to Philistines [who did not arrive in Palestine until c. 1200, the early Iron Age] and domesticated camels). Some early modern scholars of the patriarchal sagas (the accounts of Abraham, Isaac, and Jacob) sought not only to locate their historical settings but also to prove their historicity; emblematic of this approach is the work of the so-called "American School," associated with W. F. Albright and G. Ernest Wright. Funded principally by church-run schools and seminaries, these scholars practiced "biblical archaeology" in the "holy land." Today, "Near Eastern" and "Mediterranean archaeology" has primarily turned from "proving the Bible" to understanding its cultural contexts. According to Wright, the acting of God in history is central to the proclamation of Israel's faith. If the Bible were shown to be historically invalid, people might be engaging in "false faith." The American School is well known for seeking biblical parallels in documents from the ancient cities of Mari and Nuzi. Neither source, ultimately, offered confirmation of the patriarchal sagas.

While the American School was positivistic and optimistic, the early "German School" might be classified as minimalistic, more interested in literature than archaeology, in determining why the stories were told than proving their historicity. The dominant figures are Albrecht Alt and Martin Noth. Alt associated the patriarchs with clan deities: the shield of Abraham, the Fear of Isaac, and so on. Noth posited that although the patriarchs were likely historical figures, the stories were conveyed, over time, in legendary or saga-based form. The school noted etiologies (stories of origin): the explanations of such practices as circumcision and dietary regulations; natural phenomena, such as the Dead Sea and free-standing salt pillars; and such ethnic interests as the fractious relationship between Israel and Moab (Hebrew *m'av*, "from [my] father," the child conceived incestuously by Lot's daughter after she made her father drunk [Gen. 19:30–38])—a story that echoes Noah's fate and anticipates an ethnic reference that reappears strikingly in the Book of Ruth.

Arguments for a relatively early origin to several tales include the recording of patriarchal practices that were offensive to the religious sensibilities of later times. Gen. 20:12, Abraham's insistence that Sarah is both his sister and his wife, is counter to Lev. 18:9 and Deut. 27:22. Jacob, Abraham's grandson, marries two sisters, contravening Lev. 18:18. The majority of biblical scholars today date the literary composition of the patriarchal sagas to the Judean royal court, c. 900, with the writing of the "J" source. Additions continued to be made until the text reached its (more-or-less) final shape sometime in the late 5th or early 4th centuries, with a possible final editing as late as Hellenistic times.

Because the patriarchal stories concern morality, responsibility, and faith, more than just historical approaches are necessary to their understanding. Theological, ethical, and literary questions also enter the discussion. How should Hagar's first flight to the wilderness be assessed? Is God abusive or protective for sending her back? Why does the text present a major theophany (appearance of the Deity) to a woman, a foreigner, and a slave?

What does this suggest about Hebrew/Egyptian relationships?

Genesis 12, Abram's introduction, threatens to repeat the disasters of the primeval history, yet Abram not only survives but thrives. His story provokes, but does not answer, questions of human and heavenly responsibility, as close reading demonstrates. Promised "a great nation," Abram's circumstances cast doubt on the promise; he himself is very old (seventy-five at his departure, Gen. 12:4); his (only) wife, Sarai, is infertile (Gen. 11:30); and his nephew, Lot, whom he takes to Canaan (anticipating that Lot will be his heir?), separates from him (Gen. 13) and moves to Sodom. Canaan's famine prompts a sojourn in Egypt (a scene repeated by subsequent generations of Hebrews).

The Expulsion of Ishmael and his mother, Hagar.

The particulars of each scene demonstrate a capacity for characterization. About to enter Egypt, Abram tells Sarai (his first words to her), "I know well that you are a beautiful woman, and when the Egyptians see you, they will say 'this is his wife'; then they will kill me … Say you are my sister, so that it may go well with me because of you …" On what is his knowledge based? In hoping that "it may go well with me," where is Abram's concern for Sarah? Abram's theology one of trust, self-interest, or test?

The Egyptian officials praise Sarai to Pharaoh, who takes her into his harem. For "her sake," he gives Abram "sheep, oxen, male donkeys, male and female slaves, female donkeys, and camels." Does Abram intend to tell the truth? If so, when? What of Sarai? Might she appreciate palace comforts after the camps of Canaan? Why is the Egyptian ruler not named; how does he compare with other Pharaohs (the Joseph saga; the Exodus)?

God afflicts Pharaoh's house with plagues. Appalled at Abram's lie—how he discovers it is not specified—Pharaoh gives him his wife and banishes him with "all that he had"; Gen. 13:1–2 reveals Abram to have become very wealthy. Gen. 12:17 reads, *al-d'var Sarai*, "concerning the matter of Sarai" (NRSV: "because of Sarah") or, literally, "upon the word of Sarai." Did Sarai's word, to the Pharaoh or to God, ensure her release? The plagues prefigure Exodus, where also Hebrews are enslaved. The stories of Egypt and Israel are thus intertwined. The "ancestress in danger" scene is repeated with both Sarah (Gen. 20:1–18) and Rebecca (Gen. 26:6–11). The "promise motif" (cf. Gen. 13:14–17), will be fulfilled outside the Pentateuch, although it continues to be threatened—by natural disasters, military campaigns, human weakness, and as we shall see in the next lecture, even divine action. ∎

Suggested Reading

William G. Dever, *Recent Archaeological Discoveries and Biblical Research*.

Niels Peter Lemche, *Early Israel: Anthropological and Historical Studies on the Israelite Society before the Monarchy*.

Phyllis Trible, *Texts of Terror: Literary-Feminist Readings of Biblical Narratives*.

Questions to Consider

1. What evidence would convince a skeptic of the historicity of the patriarchs? Even if their existence were proven, how would one determine the historicity of the stories told about them?

2. It is often claimed that the patriarchal tales represent universal stories rather than temporally contingent ones. In what sense then are we like

Abraham, Sarah, and Hagar? If we identify with the characters, do we risk romanticizing the past?

3. Why would Israel present Abraham, its forefather, in a manner many readers find morally ambiguous?

Isaac
(Genesis 21–22)
Lecture 5

God decides to test Abraham, so he tells Abraham to take his son, Isaac, and kill him, offer him up as a burnt offering. ... It's only 19 verses. This is one of the best short stories ever written. It is so packed.

The arguments for Mosaic authorship of the Pentateuch (Greek for "five scrolls") are scripturally based, but they face numerous problems. Scripture and early commentary do suggest Mosaic authorship. The term "the Books of Moses" appears in Ezra 6:18; Exod. 24:4; Josh. 8:31; and in the Old Testament Apocrypha, Ecclus. 24:23. Attributions of Mosaic authorship are suggested by the 1st-century C.E. Jewish historian Josephus (*Ant.* 4), the Jewish philosopher Philo of Alexandria's *Life of Moses*, and in Christian sources Mark 12:26 and Acts 15:21.

Arguments against full Mosaic authorship appear already in antiquity. Fourth Ezra (2nd Esdras) records (14) that Ezra rewrote the Torah after it was destroyed. Saint Jerome, in the late 4th century, makes a similar observation. The Christian philosopher Clement of Alexandria (3rd century) denied that Moses would tell such a lie as that of Noah's drunkenness (Gen. 9). With the Enlightenment, more rigorous criticisms of Mosaic authorship appeared. Why would Moses refer to himself in the third person? Is the Deity's name Elohim, YHWH, El-Elyon, El-Shaddai? ("God" translates "elohim"; "Lord" signals the Hebrew letters "Y-H-W-H," also called the *Tetragrammaton* [Greek for "four letters"]). There are (apparent) contradictions leading to such questions as, What came first: animals (Genesis 1) or humankind (Genesis 2)? Did Noah take animals two by two or seven by seven? Was the Torah given on Mt. Sinai (Exod. 19) or Mt. Horeb (Deut. 1)? Is Moses's father-in-law Jethro, Ruel, or Hobab? Repetition in the Bible have also contributed to criticism (The Ten Commandments, or "Decalogue" (Greek: "ten words"), appear in Exodus 20 and 34 and Deuteronomy 5, with thirty minor variations. The "ancestress in danger" appears three times. The three accounts of how

Isaac received his name—Gen. 17, 18, and 21—differ as to who laughed and why.)

The divine names could reflect different aspects of the divine personality: YHWH for ethics, Elohim for transcendent manifestation. "Contradictions" may be harmonized or may result from a single author's mistake. Repetition may also represent authorial artistry, as we'll see in the next lecture.

The trial of Abraham's faith.

In 1651, Thomas Hobbes had already claimed that much of the Pentateuch was post-Mosaic; shortly thereafter, Baruch Spinoza made similar claims. The major spokesperson for this model, now called the Documentary or Graf-Welhausen Hypothesis, was Julius Welhausen, who in 1878, working with the theories of Graf, published his *Prolegomenon to the History of Ancient Israel*.

Exegesis (from the Greek for "to draw out"), or scholarly analysis, includes source criticism and the various other methods that these lectures have already adduced. The method applied determines both what questions are brought to the text and the means by which answers are derived. Our test case is Genesis 22. How do we interpret the story? Anthropology suggests the *Akedah* may be an etiology explaining why the Hebrews do not practice human sacrifice. The practice was known: Jephthah sacrifices his daughter (Jdg. 11); Ahaz and Manasseh, their sons (2 Kgs. 16 and 21, cf. Mesha King of Moab, 2 Kgs. 3:27). Ezek. 20:26 even speaks of a divine command ordering child sacrifice. Exod. 22.29–30 suggests that all first-born children and animals belong to God (cf. Exod. 24:10–20 on redeeming first-born males). To offer a child was to offer one's most precious possession (Carthage). However, Abraham is rewarded precisely *because* he is willing to offer his child.

For the Church, the *Akedah* prefigures the cross; the sacrifice of sons by fathers. Isaac carries his wood; Jesus carries his cross (Epistle of Barnabas). Jewish (Rabbinic) exegesis, sometimes considered a forerunner of deconstruction, concentrates on what is said and what is omitted. Explanation of the very detailed v. 2 in a remarkably condensed chapter. Interest in the silence between son and father. As Ishmael and Isaac face death; one is passive, the other, questioning. This introduces the motif of countering primogeniture. Hagar and Abraham both heed angelic messages: one in anguish, the other, silent. Might the *Akedah* also have been Abraham's test of God? Why does Abraham plead for Sodom but not for Isaac? Did Abraham recognize that his son's loyalty was to his mother? Gen. 23:1 notes, "Sarah died at Kiriath-Arba, that is, Hebron." But Abraham had "returned to Beersheva." Isaac brings Rebecca "into the tent of Sarah his mother"—"of Sarah his mother" is absent in some Greek manuscripts. "He took Rebecca, and she became his wife, and he loved her. So Isaac was comforted after his mother's death" (24:67).

We might wonder what effect the event had on Isaac. Compared to his father and his sons Jacob and Esau, he appears passive, weak, and repetitive, but perhaps he is more savvy than them all. The biblical stories were originally told orally, and what is conveyed—in person, through dialogue—may give quite another impression. We see this as we turn to the Jacob saga. ■

Suggested Reading

Joseph Blenkinsopp, *The Pentateuch: An Introduction to the First Five Books of the Bible*, Anchor Bible Reference Library.

Carol Lowery Delaney, *Abraham on Trial: The Social Legacy of Biblical Myth*.

Jon D. Levenson, *Death and Resurrection of the Beloved Son: The Transformation of Child Sacrifice in Judaism and Christianity*.

Shalom Spiegel, *The Last Trial*. Translated by Judah Golden.

Questions to Consider

1. What moral judgment should be made concerning Abraham? Concerning God?

2. Sacrifice was as common in antiquity as television is today. Why did it become less common, and is it something that has been replaced or should be revived?

3. Why might Judaism have chosen this passage as the New Year (Rosh ha-Shanah) reading?

The Jacob Saga
(Genesis 25–36)
Lecture 6

Form criticism is not designed to set out what is historical. Form criticism, like folktales, is designed to tell a good story using certain literary conventions that people will recognize, such as genealogies and annunciations. Close reading tells us that how that form is finally played out in terms of dialogue, plot description, juxtaposition, characterization, and motivation.

The form critic, influenced by folktale analysis, focuses on the units (*pericopae*, sing. *pericope*, from the Greek for "to cut around") that comprise the larger narrative and attempts to locate the social setting of that unit in its oral stage. The form critic seeks the "setting in life" (*Sitz-im-Leben*) of the tale before its incorporation into the biblical narrative. Form criticism notes the parameters of each *pericope*; the premise is that the stories originally circulated independently, perhaps even unconnected to the patriarchs. Although the form remains consistent, studies of oral cultures reveal that storytellers typically adapt their accounts to times, places, and audiences. The form does not, and cannot, guarantee a basis in historical fact.

Let's test this with Genesis 25; form critical observations on the stories of Jacob and Esau. The account begins with an etiology: "Two nations are in your womb, and two peoples, born of you, shall be divided; the one will outdo the other, and the older will serve the younger" (Gen. 25:23–24). Jacob (Israel) will prevail over Esau (Edom). The etiological couplet authenticates the oracle. Its relationship to earlier "annunciation" etiologies (Gen. 16:11–12) prompts comparison: Rebecca, like Hagar, is heeded by God and, again, the oracle is not entirely encouraging. Esau's description as "red and hairy" ("red": *admoni*; 25:25) connects him to Edom ("red"), one of Israel's enemies. *Seir*, "hairy," is a pun on Seir, Edomite territory (Gen. 32:3).

Literary analysis observes the effects of description (the Bible rarely provides physical description), names, and authorial remarks. "The first came forth red, his whole body like a hairy coat. So they named him Esau" (Gen. 25:25). He appears animal-like, brutish (the Gilgamesh epic describes the animalistic, uncivilized Enkidu as "wild and hairy"). He is introduced through physical features rather than action; there is little subtlety.

"Afterwards his brother came forth, and his hand had taken hold of Esau's heel, so his name was called Jacob" (25:26). The focus on action makes Jacob appear more subtle, less easy to read. He is "grasping" by nature. His name, "one who supplants," portends that he raises himself up by pulling others down. Is this name appropriate for Israel's (eponymous) ancestor? Does its change to "Israel ... who 'struggles with God' and prevails" signal changed character?

When the boys grew up, Esau was a skilled hunter, a man of the field, while Jacob was an *ish tam*—usually translated "quiet man"—dwelling in tents (25:27). Is the hunter valued or seen as uncivilized? Does "man of the field" distinguish Esau from the patriarchs or equate him with the earlier first born, Ishmael? In what sense is Jacob *tam*? The term elsewhere connotes innocence and/or moral integrity; cf. Abimelech of Gerar, who explains (Gen. 20:5–6) he is *tam* because he did not know that Sarah was Abraham's wife.

Literary criticism also attends to motive, which the Bible usually suppresses: "Isaac loved Esau because he ate his game, but Rebecca loved Jacob" (25:28). Is Isaac self-centered, thinking with his stomach—as Esau did earlier? Does the father live vicariously through his son? Does Esau remind Isaac of his beloved older brother, Ishmael? Is Rebecca's love—minus an explicit motive—self-serving? Motivated by the oracle? Does she love Jacob because she can control him? Because he is more like her? Does she love Jacob because Isaac loves Ishmael?

Literary criticism also explores the effects of dialogue: "Once when Jacob was boiling pottage, Esau came in from the field and he was famished. Esau said to Jacob, 'Let me eat some of that red pottage, for I am famished'" (25:29–30). Esau does what the narrator says, in the same terms; there is no complexity. "Let me eat some of that red pottage, for I am famished" (RSV) misses the impact of the Hebrew: "Let me chow down on that red, red stuff." Jacob responds: "First today sell your birthright [entitlement to a double portion of the estate] to me." His deliberateness contrasts Esau's breathlessness. Narrative voice reinforces Esau's lack. The Hebrew reads, literally: "And he ate, and drank, and rose, and went and despised, did Esau, the birthright" (25:34a).

Literary criticism asks (moving to ideological criticism): What are its views of those holding power? Leaders need to provide food. Esau, a hunter, was famished; Jacob had food and knew how to bargain with it. The motif reappears with Jacob's grandson, Joseph, and with Moses.

Israel's national saga depicts the community as succeeding through brains (and trickery) rather than (military) might. But success, especially through trickery, comes at a price. God enters history, although Israel can never determine when. To obey divine commands may entail personal suffering. The oracle of Israel's success over Edom waits centuries until it is fulfilled (2 Sam. 8:12–14; 2 Chr. 25:11–14); this gives the nation hope in times of distress.

Literary-critical readers finally attend to aesthetics. Although perhaps originally independent, the Jacob stories satisfy artistically through repetition of motifs and plot lines. Action and counteraction. As Jacob tricks Esau with Rebecca's help, so Jacob is tricked by Rebecca's brother Laban. Working seven years for Rachel, Jacob wakes to discover he has consummated a marriage with Leah, she of "tender eyes." Leah resembles the blind Isaac. Was Isaac similarly duped? Laban's rationale—"It is not done so in our country to give the younger before the first born" (29:26)—repays Jacob for usurping Esau's birthright and blessing.

As Jacob tricked Isaac with false garments—the skins his mother prepared—so Jacob is tricked by Joseph's coat, dipped in goat's blood. Potiphar's wife uses Joseph's coat as false evidence of his attacking her (Gen. 39). Joseph's Egyptian clothes disguise his identity from his brothers. Judah, the inheritor of the promise, is tricked when his daughter-in-law,

Tamar (Gen. 38), removes her widow's clothes and wraps herself in a veil; Judah takes her to be a prostitute and has intercourse with her.

No mere historical accounts, the patriarchal sagas raise complex issues of morality, theology, and community identity, even as they provide aesthetic delight. The following lecture, on literary conventions, is our final foray into literary criticism. ■

Suggested Reading

Robert Alter, *The Art of Biblical Narrative*.

Questions to Consider

1. To what extent are the patriarchal sagas profitably compared with folktales?

2. Can, or should, various *pericopae* in Genesis be seen as funny? What delight might the original audience have found in them? In oral presentation?

3. Do the accounts of Esau (as well as Ishmael) indicate an ambivalent relationship between Israel and its neighbors? Does Israel regard these other nations as "in the family"?

Folklore Analysis and Type Scenes
(Genesis 25–36, cont.)
Lecture 7

As we look at the Bible, it turns out that those motifs common to ... all folktales, actually show up in the Bible. The folktale analysis may be looked at as a type of form criticism.

Earlier approaches to the Bible, such as source and form criticism, find application in the study of conventional plot lines, or "type scenes." Rather than regard such repetition as indicating a retelling of a single episode by different sources, type-scene analysis shows how changes in the convention disclose narrative art, as well as convey information about community heroes and values. Because type-scene analysis owes much to the study of folklore (e.g., permutations of the Cinderella story or of modern "urban legends"), we begin with folkloric conventions. Our test case is the continuation of the Jacob saga. We then turn to type-scene analysis by examining various encounters of men and women at wells. This lecture also includes a brief foray into the Gospel of John, where another version of the type scene appears.

Folktale analysts, such as the Russian formalist Vladimir Propp, observe that traditional stories are composed of a number of set motifs. In tracing a few of Propp's motifs, our test case is the story of Jacob, beginning where the previous lecture ended, Gen. 27:41. (1) The hero is absent from home: Jacob is sent away both to escape his brother and to find a wife (Gen. 28:2,5). Abraham and Moses face similar displacements, as do Ruth, Esther, Jonah, and Daniel; their stories also are profitably interpreted as folktales. (2) Heroes are often aided by helpers. As Jacob is helped by God, so are Abraham and Moses. (3) An opponent seeks to thwart the hero. Jacob faces not only his father-in-law, Laban, and his brother Esau but also a mysterious wrestler at the Jabbok River. The number of opponents demonstrates his extreme peril, bravery, and ultimate good fortune. Moses confronts Pharaoh and his own people; David faces opposition from Saul and others. (4) The hero receives a mark or brand, usually indicating maturation or survival. "When the man saw that he did not prevail against Jacob, he touched the hollow of his thigh, and Jacob's thigh was put out of joint as he wrestled with him" (Gen. 32:25). Thereafter, he walks with a limp. Other examples include the mark of Cain (Gen. 4:15), Abraham's circumcision (Gen. 17:9–14, 23–27), and Moses's shining face (Exod. 34:29–35). And finally, (5) The hero is transfigured. As the frog becomes a prince, so Jacob is told (Gen. 32:28): "Your name shall no more be called Jacob, but Israel, for you have striven with God and with people, and have prevailed."

Jacob wrestling with the angel.

Recognizing the formulaic, audiences delight in the manipulation of details (hence, the popularity of situation comedies, game shows, teen slasher films). Although the Bible likely contains singular examples of what its original audiences would have recognized to be conventions, some cases remain evident, including birth annunciations, the "ancestress in danger," infertile women becoming pregnant, and perhaps the entire Book of Judges. Our test case, the meeting of a woman at a well, begins with a comparison of Gen. 29 (Jacob meets Rachel) and Gen. 24 (Abraham's servant meets Rebecca) and includes Moses (Exod. 2) and Saul (1 Sam. 9).

The pattern opens: The hero leaves home to find a wife. Gen. 24 offers the first break in the convention: Rather than Isaac, Abraham's servant fills the hero role. The story reinforces Isaac's passivity and confirms his association with substitutes: the ram at the *Akedah*, Rebecca's filling the gap caused by Sarah's death, the switching of the blessing. Unlike Abraham's servant, who travels with camels and gifts, Jacob leaves without money, fleeing his brother. He makes his own way in the world. Similarly, fleeing Egypt, Moses arrives at a well in Midian (Exod. 2:15b–21). Moses stumbles into fate rather than proactively engaging it; he is not planning on finding a wife, any more than finding a burning bush or freeing his people. Saul goes to a well not to find a wife but his father's donkeys (1 Sam. 9:11–12). Jesus goes to Jacob's well, meets a Samaritan woman, and discusses marriage with her (John 4).

The next step: The man meets the woman. Arriving at the well, Abraham's servant prays for matchmaking success; only this variant, in which the man is not explicitly a Hebrew, is marked by religiosity. Jacob, ever the negotiator, begins by speaking to the townsmen. This scene foreshadows Gen. 34, the rape of his daughter Dinah, in which Jacob is again more attentive to political alliances between men than to emotional alliances with women. Moses arrives at the well before the women. There, he meets not men, but the seven—indistinguishable—daughters of a Midianite priest. Moses's life will continue to revolve more around priestly than domestic matters. Saul meets a group of women. Rather than aiding the women, as Jacob and Moses do, Saul is helped by the women on the very banal question of those lost donkeys. Thus, from the beginning, Saul is dependent on others. His relationship with women is a minor theme; where it sounds, such as with his daughter Michal, who betrays him with David, it is generally negative. Jesus too meets a woman, but his initial interest in obtaining drinking water flows into a discussion of "living water."

Third, the hero obtains water. Rebecca draws water for Abraham's servant and for his camels. Her energy contrasts with Isaac's passivity. Gen. 24:16–20 makes her the subject of eleven active verbs. The recounting of this meeting is, like the water, drawn out: a complex introduction fitting Rebecca's complex character. The narrator adds that she is "beautiful and a virgin"; we know nothing of Isaac's appearance, let alone sexual status. In contrast to Rebecca, Rachel does little. Jacob draws the water and only after removing the stone over the well. The stone is Jacob's signature: he is, as Robert Alter puts it, "a man who sleeps on stones, speaks in stones, wrestles with stones, contending with the hard, unyielding nature of things, whereas in pointed contrast his favored son will make his way in the world as a dealer in the truths intimated through the filmy insubstantiality of dreams." Like Jacob, Moses faces blocks; in this case, hostile shepherds. For Moses, nothing comes easy and enemies arise from all quarters. Moreover, Moses does more than help the women; he "saves" (*hoshea*) them. Saul obtains neither water nor bride. To the contrary, he gets information about a local "seer"—the prophet Samuel. His dependence on Samuel remains throughout his tragic story. Saul leaves the well in search of donkeys; like his kingship, his type scene is aborted. It may be telling that Saul's successor, David, never participates in this type scene; he is "unconventional." Jesus never gets water from the woman; instead, he provides her "living water."

Fourth, the marriage is contracted. Laban notices the bracelets, anklets, and nose-ring Rebecca received. The family learns that Isaac is Abraham's only heir—he's the best catch in the Middle East. We might speculate on what motivates the family agreeing to the marriage, just as we might speculate about Rebecca's motives in favoring Jacob. It is Rebecca, not her father or her brother, who makes the final decision. Rachel's beauty is not mentioned until the discussion of marriage, where it is commodified in connection to the bride price. To possess Rachel, Jacob has to bargain, as he had earlier done with Esau. Complicating the situation is Rachel's older sister, Leah, of "weak" (or "tender") eyes. Is Leah like Isaac: more victim than actor? Will she too be passed over, less loved? Moses is encouraged to marry by the Midianite priest Jethro; Moses frequently needs to be prompted. Jethro will later give Moses guidance on community governance (Exod. 18:14–27). No marriage takes place between Jesus and the Samaritan. The woman, married numerous times, is currently living with, although not married to, a man.

Folktales and type scenes are told less (if at all) for the sake of historicity. They are typically presented as events attested by unconfirmed witnesses. They assume different facets as they move from teller to teller, culture to culture. They reveal more about cultural and character-based issues than about "what really happened." They can also influence the presentation of history, because "what really happened" can be conformed to the plot. Folktales and type scenes are not necessarily either easily recognized or easily classified. Identification becomes increasingly difficult when the accounts are more complex and the points of contact are less clear. An excellent example is "the Jew in the court of the foreign king."

Given what we've covered so far, the story of Moses to which we now turn should already be somewhat familiar. A child, like Isaac, is born under special circumstances; a people, like Sarah in Pharaoh's harem, is enslaved in Egypt; plagues brought upon Pharaoh and his house encourage him to free his captives; the hand of God shows fidelity to Moses in the covenant made with the patriarchs; the story includes the presence of strong—and tricky—women; it contains unexpected humor; and as in Genesis, it contains great pathos. ■

Suggested Reading

Robert Alter, *The Art of Biblical Narrative*.

Alan Dundes, *Holy Writ as Oral Lit: The Bible as Folklore*.

Susan Niditch, *Folklore and the Hebrew Bible*.

Questions to Consider

1. How do the annunciation scenes (Abraham, Hagar, Rebecca, Samson's mother [Elizabeth, Mary]) reveal different aspects of characterization?

2. Why are so many type scenes connected with women?

Moses and Exodus
(Exodus 1–15)
Lecture 8

> **There is nothing in the Egyptian records nor in any other records. If I were an Egyptian record keeper, the escape of a group of slaves from my troops is not something I would care to record. Moreover, this group of slaves might have actually been quite small, but the Bible has increased the numbers and increased the importance. Whether historical or not, we simply can't prove it.**

Slavery in Egypt: Although Hebrew slavery in Egypt is unnoted in external sources, slavery itself in the ancient Near East is well attested, and Genesis anticipates the Egyptian circumstances. Sometimes, ancient bondage was less what we think of as slavery than a kind of extended forced labor, or *corvee*. An inscription from Thutmosis II (c. 1490–1436 B.C.E.) depicting Asiatics engaged in brick work has the taskmaster say, "The rod is in my hand; do not be idle." The Egyptian poem "Satire on the Trades" describes the brick-worker: "He is dirtier than vines or pigs from treading under his mud. His clothes are stiff with clay ... He is miserable ... His sides ache ... His arms are destroyed. He washes himself only once a season. He is simply wretched through and through."

Egyptian slavery fulfills patriarchal predictions and, thereby, indicates that nothing has gone awry with God's promises to the patriarchs. The Lord said to Abram, "Know for certain that your descendants will be sojourners in a land which is not theirs, and will be slaves there, and they will be oppressed for four-hundred years" (Gen. 15:13–14). The Egyptian slave Hagar is, with her son Ishmael, exiled—with anticipation of death—into the wilderness. The Ishmaelites sell Joseph into slavery, and the Egyptians enslave Sarah's descendants and threaten their sons. The Pharaoh "who knew not Joseph" is, like the pharaohs encountered by Abraham and Jacob's sons, unidentified. (The title, meaning "Great house," is a metonymy, cf. "The White House announced

... .") The absence of the name may result from *damnatio memoriae*, the erasing of a name from history (cf. The monotheistically inclined Amenhotep [Ikhnaton]). The omission enhances theological implications. Ancient Egyptians viewed Pharaoh as divine; a contest between God and Pharaoh opposes rival claimants for divinity. It enhances folkloric connections.

Text criticism also complicates the story. This approach attempts to determine the earliest literary version; it is applied often in cases where the Hebrew (MT) and Greek (LXX) accounts differ. The Hebrew of Exod. 1:22 reads: "Then Pharaoh commanded his people, 'Every son that is born you shall cast into the Nile.'" The Septuagint, Targums, and Samaritan Pentateuch add "[born] *to the Hebrews*." The conventional wisdom in text criticism is that the more difficult reading (*lectio difficilior*) is likely to be original. The additional detail included in the Septuagint appears to be a later clarification; it is easy to determine why it was added, but less so why it may have been deliberately removed. The more indeterminate Hebrew heightens Pharaoh's ineptitude.

Ironically, several women—Moses's mother and sister; the Pharaoh's daughter, along with the midwives Shiphra and Puah—through deception, subvert royal power. The midwives confirm Pharaoh's view of the Hebrews as "other" than normal. By adopting the child, Pharaoh's daughter flouts her father's order. Moses's sister arranges for him to be nursed (for wages) by his own mother. Moses's initial display of his commission is a simple magic trick: Aaron's staff becomes a snake (Exod. 7:8–13); the court magicians perform the same trick, only to have their staffs swallowed by Aaron's. The magicians also turn water into blood (Exod. 7:22), hardly what Egypt needed.

But what about Moses? His early life, also unattested in Egyptian sources, evokes cross-cultural folktales and Israelite cosmogonic motifs. His infancy parallels that of Sargon of Akkad: protected by women from execution by an evil king, placed in a reed basket, and rescued. The term for Moses's basket is the same for Noah's ark (*tevah*). And Moses escapes drowning, as does Noah.

Moses's initial action opens the folktale motif of the hero's leave-taking. Moses's self-imposed exile is prompted initially not by Egyptians but by Hebrew slaves aware of the taskmaster's murder. Moses flees from Pharaoh, who "sought to kill" him (Exod. 2:15). The motif is repeated when Moses returns to Egypt (Exod. 4:24–26), but the Lord is the agent of death. Again, Moses is rescued by a woman, his wife, Zipporah, by apotropaic magic. Foreshadowed are both Moses's breaking the power of slavemasters and his struggles with the slave generation.

The finding of Moses.

Although the ten plagues have received "scientific" explications (earthquakes; Atlantis [!]), the biblical text is interested not in rationales but in divine power. Inclined after each plague to free the slaves, Pharaoh has a "change of heart." In Exod. 4:14, ten times Pharaoh hardens his heart; ten times God prompts this change. Biblical Hebrew associates emotions with physiology: Jeremiah (4:19) cries: "My bowels, my bowels, I writhe in pain!" (RSV: "My anguish! My anguish!"). "In the night my heart instructs me" (RSV, Ps. 16:7); the Hebrew is "My kidneys afflict me." The hardening of the heart is the ossification of one's vital principle. It indicates, as Nahum Sarna eloquently observes, "a state of moral atrophy."

Theologians wrestle with the question of morality. Some explain the apparent contradiction between Pharaoh's action and divine responsibility as expressing the intractable problem of fate and free will. Others note that Pharaoh had established himself as callous and inconsistent. God then prompts him to manifest his true self. The Bible has its own explanation.

Exod. 10:1–2 (cf. Exod. 9:15–16): "Then the Lord God said to Moses, 'Go in to Pharaoh, for I have hardened his heart and the hearts of his servants, that I may show these signs of mine among them.'" "And that you may tell in the hearing of your children, and your children's children how I have toyed with the Egyptians and what signs I have done among them, that you may know that I am the Lord." God responds not only out of compassion, then, but also because of remembering the covenant he made with the Hebrew people.

Exodus culminates with the splitting of the sea and the escape of Israelites and others. "Reed Sea" (LXX, "Red Sea") may explain the miracle: The Hebrews escaped through marshes, but Egyptian chariots got stuck in the mud. The word for "reed" is the same as the material of Moses's basket. His escape from watery death had prefigured the Exodus.

Theologically and ethically, Israelite existence is interpreted through the Exodus. Deut. 5:15 (cf. Exod. 20:11): "Remember that you were a slave in the land of Egypt, and the Lord your God brought you out from there with a mighty hand and an outstretched arm; therefore remember the Lord your God commanded you to keep the Sabbath day." Exod. 22:21 (cf. Deut. 23:7): "You shall not wrong a stranger or oppress him, for you were strangers in the land of Egypt." Deut. 24:17–18: "You shall not subvert the rights of the fatherless ... remember that you were a slave in the land of Egypt and that the Lord your God redeemed you." ∎

Suggested Reading

Jonathan Kirsch, *Moses: A Life.*

Göran Larsson, *Bound for Freedom: The Book of Exodus in Jewish and Christian Traditions.*

Questions to Consider

1. What is the moral vision of this material, given Moses's killing of the taskmaster and hiding the body and God's hardening of Pharaoh's heart? Do the Egyptians "get what they deserve"? Does anyone "deserve" the death of a child?

2. To what extent is Aaron highlighted in the story, and how do those episodes reflect priestly (P) interests?

3. Is there any means to distinguish "fact" from "fiction" in this narrative?

The God of Israel
(Exodus 1–15, cont.)
Lecture 9

> This God responds to Moses: "Ehyeh asher ehyeh." "I am what I am" … This is a God of being, a God of process, a God of future orientation. A God who takes whatever form this God wants to take. … Subsequently, whenever this God is referred to, … he is referred to, as "YHWH," which actually translates the Hebrew, "He will be" or "He is what He is."

More than an account of the liberation of Hebrew slaves, the opening chapters of Exodus also provide insight into the name of the Deity and the sources used in the Pentateuch's composition. When Moses is told to rescue his people, he asks (Exod. 3:13), "If I come to the people of Israel and say to them, 'The god of your fathers has sent me to you,' and they ask me, 'What is his name?' what shall I say to them?" In other words, "Which god are you?" The question makes excellent sense in the polytheistic Near East. The voice responds with a name both cryptic and revelatory, "I will be what I will be." The Deity's name is given in Exod. 3:14, and only here, in the first person, *ehyeh asher ehyeh*, meaning both "I will be what I will be" and "I am what I am." All other Hebrew references appear in the third person form: "he will be" (YHWH). Into Greek, the active "I will be" becomes the static "I am" (*ego eimi*).

Sometimes called the *Tetragrammaton* (Greek meaning "four letters"), YHWH is composed of four consonants (early Hebrew manuscripts lack vowels). The name eventually received vowels (called "points") taken from the Hebrew for "my Lord," *Adonai*. This resulted in the term "YaHoWaH," which gives us, finally, "Jehovah." The *Tetragrammaton* was probably pronounced by the Hebrew priests. Legend has it that the name, attributed with increasing holiness, came to be recited once a year, on Yom Kippur (the Day of Atonement), by the high priest in the Holy of Holies of the Jerusalem Temple, at the moment that chanting from the Temple choir swelled.

Readings of the *Tanakh*, as well as prayers in Judaism, substitute the Hebrew "My Lord" (*Adonai*) for the *Tetragrammaton*. Some Jews will even provide circumlocutions for *Adonai* (e.g., *ha-Shem* ["the name"]) to preserve the holiness of the name. The Jewish mystical tradition asserts that the name is ineffable; were it to be correctly pronounced, says one legend, the Messiah would come. Other writers speak of myriad pronunciations.

In Hebrew culture, names are more than labels. To "call one's name" or to know one's name signals power. Given mastery over the woman, Adam "calls her name Eve" (Gen. 3:20). A name change signals a change in one's fate and the fate of one's descendants—Sarai to Sarah ("princess"), Jacob to Israel. Etymologies provide insight into character and fate. Isaac is "laughter"; Israel is "one who strives with God"; and Jacob is "supplanter."

Hebrew words are typically built on tri-consonantal roots (stems). Analogous would be the root SNG, whence: sing, sang, song. The root of YHWH is that the root is unclear. The most common derivation is from the root meaning "to be, become, make happen." This future emphasis matches Hebrew's verbal orientation. It fits embedded uses of the term, such as Exod. 6:6–8, "I am YHWH, and I will bring you out from under the burdens of the Egyptians, and I will deliver you from bondage, and I will redeem you with an outstretched arm and with great acts of judgment. And I will take you for my people, and I will be your god, and you shall know that I am YHWH …" A second possibility is the root for "to fall." The connotations are both to make a sudden appearance, like a meteor, and to cause rain to fall. This derivation would strengthen the connection of YHWH to Near Eastern storm and nature gods, such as the Canaanite Baal. The name may have originated as "Yah," a battle cry. Perhaps the origin is deliberately vague or overdetermined: YHWH is never fully known.

Even were we to locate the name's origin, it may yield little about the origins of YHWHism. For this question, we return to source criticism. According to Exod. 3:16, usually assigned to E (Elohist, Ephraimite), YHWH ("Lord") appears first at the burning bush. Earlier, the deity was "Elohim" (God). Exod. 3:1 locates the bush on Mt. Horeb, another term (probably E) for Mt. Sinai. The Hebrew for the "bush" is (ironically?), *Sineh*, like "Sinai."

The Israelites resemble the bush: small but invincible; threatened but never consumed; humble, yet strong. Gen. 4:26–27 quotes Eve at the birth of Seth: "God [Elohim] has appointed for me another child instead of Abel ... To Seth also was born a son, and he called his name Enosh. At that time, people began to call upon the name of the Lord [YHWH]." This verse, in possible contradiction to Exod. 3, is usually assigned to J. And finally the priestly (P) commentary is found in Exod. 6:2, which observes, "God [Elohim] said to Moses, 'I am YHWH. I appeared to Abraham, Isaac, and Jacob as El Shaddai ["god of the mountain"; perhaps, "of the breasts"; cf. Gen. 17:1] but my name YHWH I did not make known to them.'"

Perhaps in its earliest cultic history, Israel's chief deity was El (generic "god") not YHWH; later, the two were assimilated. "Israel" is based on "el," not "YHWH." Deut. 32:8–9 casts YHWH as one of El's sons: "When the most high (Elyon) gave to the nations their inheritance, when he separated humanity, he fixed the boundaries of peoples according to the number of divine beings. For YHWH's portion is his people, Jacob his allotted heritage." Characteristics of the Canaanite sky-god El are assimilated to YHWH. Ugaritic and Canaanite texts depict El as an elderly, bearded man enthroned in a divine council. So, too, YHWH is sometimes depicted (Ps. 102; Job 36; Isa. 40; Dan. 7:9, and so on) as an aged patriarch, enthroned in a divine assembly (1 Kgs. 22; Isa. 6: Ps. 29, 82, and so on).

Theories of the cult's origin are similarly complex. The "Kenite hypothesis" suggests that the Israelites learned of YHWH, the god of Mt. Sinai, from Moses's father-in-law, the Midianite priest. Exod. 18:12: "Jethro, Moses' father-in-law, took a burnt offering and sacrificed it to Elohim; and Aaron came with all the elders of Israel to eat bread with Moses' father-in-law." Thus, the Kenite Jethro hosts a cultic meal. Cross-cultural influence is likely during the period of settlement: Judges 1:16 notes, "The descendants of the Kenites, Moses' father-in-law, went up with the people of Judah ... into the wilderness of Judah, which lies in the Negev near Arad, and they went and settled with the people." In Judges 4–5, the heroine Jael is married to a Kenite. First Chronicles 2:55, although a late source, associates the Kenites with the Rechabites, a group known for rigorous personal piety. Countering this view: theophoric (god-bearing) names associated with YHWH appear before Exodus 3; for example, Moses's mother Yocheved ("YHWH is glory"). But the name may be a later insertion; Exod. 2, her introduction, records no name.

Another explication returns to the theory of the patriarchs as independent clan heads: YHWH is the patron of Moses's clan, cf. Shield of Abraham (Gen. 15:1); Mighty One of Jacob (Gen. 49:24). Clan gods may have been attractive to semi-nomadic peoples whose identity is more determined by family than by land. This thesis could also explicate the first words the Deity speaks to Moses: "I am the god of your father" (Exod. 3:6). Exod. 15:2, the very old "Song of Moses": "Yah [Hebrew shortened form] is my strength and my song, he has become my salvation. This is my God and I will praise him, my father's God and I will exalt him."

The covenant community told their God's story less through etymologies or cosmologies than through recounting divine actions in history, and they described their relationship to this Deity through covenants, as the next lecture demonstrates. ■

Suggested Reading

Samuel E. Ballentine, *The Torah's Vision of Worship*.

Walter Brueggemann, *Theology of the Old Testament: Testimony, Dispute, Advocacy*.

Mark Smith, *The Early History of God: Yahweh and Other Deities in Ancient Israel*.

Questions to Consider

1. What would "wrongful use of the name of the Lord your God" (Exod. 20:7) be?

2. YHWH is sometimes considered a wilderness deity, found on Mt. Sinai in the desert. What changes in YHWH's presentation occur as the Israelites build YHWH a temple in Jerusalem?

3. Why is YHWH not imaged? Why are images (idols) in general forbidden (Exod. 20:4)?

Covenant and Law, Part I
(Exodus 19–40, Leviticus, Deuteronomy)
Lecture 10

One of the major ways that the Israelites related to their God is through covenants.

The Hebrew term for "covenant," Berit, may be familiar through such organizations as B'Nai B'rith, literally "children of the covenant." A covenant is a contract, a legal agreement between parties. The prophet Jeremiah speaks of "the new covenant" written on people's hearts (Jer. 31:31–34). The Greek expression for this contract, he kaine diatheke, is also the expression "New Testament." The Hebrew expression for "covenant making" is c'rat berit, literally, "to cut a covenant," as in the English idiom "to cut a deal." The "sign of the covenant" is circumcision, a ceremony even today in Judaism known as the Berit (Bris, in Eastern European pronunciation), Milah, "covenant of circumcision," or simply Berit.

The *Tanakh* provides two forms of covenants. The "vassal or suzerainty treaty" formulation underlies the covenant at Sinai (the Mosaic covenant, or the covenant mediated through Moses). The "royal grant" model is associated with the covenants to Noah, Abraham, and David (cf. Psalms 50, 81, 89, 32). Both forms are explicated by what may be called an "I-Thou" relationship or contracts between unequals: lord and vassal, humanity and God. The terms of the contract are binding on both parties. The two models are attested in ancient Mesopotamia from over 4,500 years ago. The Hittites, an Asiatic group, used Akkadian (Semitic) covenantal models, which may suggest that the form originated in the Mesopotamian basin. The earliest extant example is the Stele of the Vultures; this text, written before 2500 B.C.E., charmingly depicts vultures devouring corpses of the covenant party's enemy.

The covenantal form has six primary parts, each attested in biblical material. The first part, the *preamble* opens with the titles of the superior party. This appears at the opening of the Decalogue (literally, "ten words"): "I am the

Lord your God" (Exod. 20:2a). The second part, the *historical prologue* assures the party of the second part (Israel) that the party of the first part (God) can fulfill the contractual terms (typically, protection from invasion, economic alliance). In royal grants, the prologue delineates the reasons both for the vassal's obligations to the king and for the king's desire to reward the vassal. The historical prologue appears next in the Decalogue: "Who brought you out of the land of Egypt, out of the house of bondage" (Exod. 20:2b). God's motivation for freeing the people was the covenant obligation to Abraham, not, *pace* many theologians, the injustice of slavery itself.

Moses coming down from Mount Sinai.

The third part, *regulations/ stipulations* make up the third and typically the longest section. These delineate the responsibilities of the co-signatories. Treaties typically insist that the second party (the vassal) show loyalty only to the lord and avoid additional alliances. Exod. 20:3–6 mandates, "You shall have no other gods before me; you shall not make for yourself a graven image, or any likeness of anything that is in heaven above, or that is in the earth beneath, or that is in the water under the earth; you shall not bow down to them or serve them." In this third section, the Mosaic code presents a relatively uncommon element. Ancient Near Eastern covenants typically present *casuistic* ("cause-and-effect") law; that is, they list crime and punishment. The Babylonian Code of Hammurabi (from the time to which Abraham is dated), for example, offers (ll. 142–43): "If a woman so hated her husband that she has declared, 'you

47

may not have me,' her record shall be investigated at her city council; if she was careful and not at fault, even though her husband has been going out and disparaging her greatly, that woman, without incurring any blame at all, may take her dowry and go off to her father's house. If she was not careful, but a gadabout, thus neglecting her house and humiliating her husband, they shall throw that woman into the water." The Decalogue's formula is *apodictic*: command apart from result. "You shall not murder; you shall not commit adultery; you shall not steal; you shall not bear false witness against your neighbor; you shall not covet your neighbor's wife, or his manservant, or his maidservant, or his ox, or his ass, or anything else that is your neighbor's" (Exod. 20:13–17). The Mosaic code also has a proportionally higher number of positive injunctions than its ancient Near Eastern counterparts. More than a list of "thou shalt nots," it contains a fair number of "thou shalts": "Remember the Sabbath day and keep it holy. Six days you shall labor and do all your work; but the seventh day is a sabbath to the Lord your God; in it you shall not do any work: you, or your son, or your daughter, your manservant, your maidservant, or your cattle, or the sojourner who is within your gate … Honor your father and your mother …" (Exod. 20:8–12). And finally in the stipulations section, vassal/suzerainty treaties concentrate on the vassal's obligations (here, injunctions placed on Israel) in surety for future service and loyalty. The royal grant, associated with Noah, Abraham, and David, stresses the Lord's obligations in responding to loyalty shown by the vassal. Typically, this formulation involves the granting of land. In the Bible, it includes guarantees of safety from universal destruction (Noah); promises of land, descendants, and blessing (Abraham); and promises of an eternal throne (David).

The next set of covenantal forms is not included in the Decalogue proper. Part four requires the safe *deposit* of the contract and regular *public readings*. Deut. 10:5 specifically mentions depositing the tablets of the law in the Ark of the Covenant. Deut. 31:9–13 offers provisions for recitation: "At the end of every seven years, at the set time of the year of release, at the Feast of Booths [Tabernacles], when all Israel comes to appear before the Lord your God at the place which he will choose, you shall read this law before all Israel in their hearing. Assemble the people—men, women, and little ones, and the sojourner within your towns—that they may hear and learn to fear the Lord your God, and be careful to do all the words of this law." Other examples include Joshua 24 is a covenant renewal ceremony and Ezra giving a public reading "before the assembly, both men and women and all who could hear with understanding ... and the ears of all the people were attentive to the Book of the Law" (Neh. 8:2–3).

The fifth primary part of covenants—like all legal contracts—list *witnesses*. Usually the witnesses are the gods of the co-signatories. Given Israel's lack of other gods, the Bible improvises: Josh. 24:22 has the people function as both signatories and witnesses. Josh. 24:27 uses natural phenomena: "And Joshua ... took a great stone, and set it up under the oak in the sanctuary of the Lord. And Joshua said to all the people: 'Behold! This stone shall be a witness against us, for it has heard all the words of the Lord which he spoke to us.'"

And finally the last section introduces *blessings* on those who abide by the covenantal terms and *curses* on those who forsake them. These materials fulfill what is implied in apodictic formulations. Deut. 28:1 promises, "If you obey the voice of the Lord your God, being careful to do all the commandments ... blessed will you be in the city and blessed will you be in the field." Deut. 28:15ff. warns, "If you do not obey the voice of the Lord your God or be careful to do all his commandments ... cursed shall you be in the city, and cursed shall you be in the field ... in all that you undertake to do, until you are destroyed and perish quickly ... The Lord will smite you with the boils of Egypt, and with the ulcers, and the scurvy, and the itch of which you cannot be healed ..." As in Leviticus (19:18), "You shall love your neighbor as yourself," the responsibilities of the suzerain are to the weakest in the community.

The specific laws concerning morality, diet, marriage, and so on, as we see in the next lecture, ensure the covenant community's status as a holy—or separate—people, as vassals to the Lord their God. ■

Suggested Reading

Rolf Rendtorff, *The Covenant Formula: An Exegetical and Theological Investigation*, Margaret Kohl, trans.

Questions to Consider

1. Is it correct to claim that Judaism prioritizes the Mosaic (suzerainty/vassal) model and Christianity, the royal grant? As used in the biblical narrative, are these forms in tension, complementary, or both?

2. What are the possible implications for worship if the believing community is related to its Deity by contract?

3. How would the biblical suzerainty contract, or apodictic laws, be enforced?

Covenant and Law, Part II
(Exodus 20–35, Leviticus)
Lecture 11

I hope through this to be able to show the distinction between covenant and law, and why translating Torah instruction as law is probably not as accurate as we might want.

Although the extent to which this comparison works is debated, the following distinctions in purpose, sanctions, geographical limits, temporal focus, and solemnity presented originally by George Mendenhall (*The Tenth Generation*) remain provocative. *Purpose.* Covenants create new relationships in accordance with previously established stipulations (e.g., a marriage contract, a mortgage). Individuals may choose to participate. In contrast, laws regulate existing relationships. One does not, for example, have a choice about whether to participate in the U.S. legal code. One enters the covenant via assent and often by external signs (e.g., public pledge); in a legal system, one is "in" as soon as one enters the territory it governs. For Scripture, the sign is (male) circumcision: a symbol of fertility and maturity, as in the expression "circumcised fruit trees" (trees mature enough for harvesting). Women are exempted from this sign; Scripture likely sees woman's identity as a component of family identity.

In covenantal systems, rewards and punishments are meted out by the suzerain or the suzerain's agents; in Scripture, this usually means divine blessings and curses. Under law, punishment is defined and administered by the state. The covenant model, especially as Deuteronomy presents it, has inevitable problems with *theodicy* (literally, "justice of God"; the issue of why the good suffer and the wicked prosper), because it implies that the good life indicates righteous living; suffering suggests a proximate cause, such as evil behavior. The Book of Job challenges this view. Legal models typically lack reward or blessing. One is punished for disobeying the law but not—manifestly—rewarded for obedience.

Geographically, covenants are unlimited; consequently, one can live within covenantal and legal systems simultaneously. Laws are territorially bound. Where the general principle is that the "law of the state is the law" (e.g., Hebrews must obey the laws of Egypt when in Egypt), covenantal stipulations prevail in cases of conflict (as the Book of Daniel 1–6 demonstrates).

Covenants are also primarily *future-oriented* and may be regarded as solemn promises (again, cf. the marriage analogy, "in sickness and in heath"). Conversely, laws have a past orientation. We do not typically reflect on the fact of our existence in a legal system but rather note this existence when the law is broken and we are caught. The future orientation of laws exists only insofar as courts have standards for punishments, yet even here the future orientation has a past component; that is, the standards are also designed to function as deterrents.

The *solemnity* of the covenant, but not law, is marked by ritual (again, cf. marriage). For three days at Sinai, the people remained in a state of ritual purity: they washed their clothes, did not engage in sexual intercourse, and observed: "Whoever touches the mountain shall be put to death. No hand shall touch him, but he shall be stoned or shot ..." (Exod. 19:10ff.). The covenant is established in a theophany: "Mt. Sinai was wrapped in smoke, because the Lord descended upon it in a fire ... and the whole mountain quaked greatly" (Exod. 19:18). The ritual of rereading and reaffirming the covenant also differs from the legal system, where the laws remain "on the books" and are recited not for public assent, but in cases where they are challenged (e.g., the Senate) or broken (e.g., the court).

In a legal system, one either obeys the laws or suffers consequences mandated by the state. In the covenantal system, one chooses to obey. Some Christian theologies hold that biblical laws are an (ineffective) means for earning salvation. However, Jewish texts from that early period until today do not follow such a view; indeed, the covenantal model precludes it. Covenantal stipulations (*mitzvot*) do not earn one standing or election: standing or election are presupposed. One obeys commandments because one is a member of the covenant community.

Among the most well known of the so-called "ritual" laws (see Lev. 11) are those of diet (Hebrew: *Kashrut*, cf. the expression "keeping kosher"). For example, the following are forbidden: Animals that do not chew the cud and have a split hoof (e.g., pigs, rabbits, camels); animals that live in water but lack fins and scales (e.g., shellfish, crustaceans); animals that eat carrion (e.g., vultures); and anything containing blood (see Lev. 17:10–14; 19:26). Other ritual laws include: Injunctions against planting a field with two types of crops (Lev. 19:19), injunctions against wearing a garment made of two different materials (Lev. 19:19), injunctions against cross-breeding animals (Lev. 19:19), and prohibitions against tattoos and scarification (Lev. 19:28).

But where do such laws come from? Dietary and comparable regulations are normal aspects of culture and religion. Religious systems do not divorce bodies (what enters, what leaves) from the holy. All cultures maintain dietary parameters regarding what is permitted, required, or expected (e.g., the Eucharist, matzah, turkey on Thanksgiving) and what is forbidden or avoided: (e.g., blood, certain meat [in the United States, dogs, cats, rats, horses], human flesh).

Such regulations can be explained. The laws have a salutary component for one's health. Pork causes trichinosis if undercooked; shellfish frequently are diseased or cause allergic reactions. However, other ancient Near Eastern peoples were also aware of cooking procedures, and this rationale does not encompass the majority of the laws. Other rationale for the regulations could include the following. Economic reasons: Pigs are expensive to raise and contribute little in return. This rationale hardly fits laws forbidding rabbit. Syncretism: Israelites are enjoined against Canaanite (i.e., pagan) cult practices, such as the sacrifice of pigs. Again, this rationale is insufficient; Canaanites also sacrificed and ate sheep, goats, and bulls. Allegory: As the Jewish philosopher Philo of Alexandria proposed in the 1st century C.E., we avoid pig, lest we hog resources; we are like sheep, not vultures. The model is not comprehensive; camels are forbidden, but why not be camel-like and conserve resources? Or some regard injunctions as arbitrary forms of self-discipline. Most anthropologists argue that taboos are consistent across categories. A coherent explanation would consider what the dietary injunctions have in common with other laws, such as those listed above.

With some modification, the model proposed by anthropologist Mary Douglas offers a start: "Holiness requires that individuals ... conform to the class to which they belong." The classifications may be partially arbitrary, but they are relatively consistent. Animals appropriate to the water have fins and scales; animals that live in the water but lack these characteristics—shellfish, crustaceans—are forbidden. Permitted mammals are ruminants with a split hoof. Pigs lack one; camels, the other. Blood is a sign of life; animals to be eaten are dead. The combination creates a category confusion. Concern for separation and taxonomy explains planting and clothing regulations. Separation is connected to wholeness, and wholeness is connected to holiness.

The interest in avoiding category confusion extends to sexuality, including homosexuality: "You shall not lie with a male as with a female; it is an abomination. You shall not lie with any beast and defile yourself with it; neither shall any woman give herself to a beast to lie with it; it is a perversion" (Lev. 18:22–23; cf. Lev. 20:13). Are the laws intended to prevent participation in Canaanite cults? There is no clear evidence homosexuality marked Canaanite worship. To cast sexual aspersions on one's enemy is a common form of *maladicta*.

Homosexuality is forbidden because it entails misuse of semen. One locus of the argument, the story of Onan in Gen. 38, falters: Onan practiced *coitus interruptus* for birth control. A second locus are laws stating that anyone with a seminal emission is ritually impure until appropriate actions (e.g., a bath) are taken and time passes (cf. Lev. 15). Yet one is also impure—which is not a "sin"—after heterosexual intercourse. The third locus, Sodom and Gomorrah (Gen. 19), concerns violence (the Sodomites seek to "know" [here, "to rape"] the strangers). The threat concerns the assertion of power by "feminizing" the strangers (as is stereotypically associated today, for example, with prisons and prep schools). The main concern seems to be violence rather than homosexual acts. Other forms of "wasting seed"—masturbation, oral or anal (heterosexual) intercourse, intercourse with pregnant or menopausal women—are not forbidden. Category confusion again provides a helpful explication: A man who lies with "a male as with a female" puts the male in the woman's role. Lesbianism is omitted (but see Rom. 1) likely because for the Israelite, sexual intercourse was defined as involving penile penetration.

A few of the many other notable texts in the legal corpus include: The only "trial by ordeal" is the "test of bitter waters" (Num. 5:11–31), designed to appease a man overcome by a "spirit of jealousy" in suspecting his wife of adultery. Moral laws encompass the majority of the *Mitzvot*: care for the poor and the stranger, justice in the courts, honesty in the marketplace, peace in the family, and so on. Israelite tradition did not distinguish between "ritual" and "moral" laws. Both were mandated by the Deity as parts of the covenant. Both enabled the people to be "holy." Finally, we come to the laws concerning holy war. For these we turn to the Book of Deuteronomy (Deut. 20–21) and to the Deuteronomic History, which begins with the Book of Joshua, a book of war. ■

Suggested Reading

Mary Douglas, *Purity and Danger: An Analysis of Concepts of Pollution and Taboo*.

Howard Eilberg-Schwartz, *The Savage in Judaism: An Anthropology of Israelite Religion and Judaism*.

Victor H. Matthews, Bernard Levinson, and Tikva Frymer-Kensky, *Gender and Law in the Hebrew Bible and the Ancient Near East*.

Saul Olyan, *Rites and Rank: Hierarchy in Biblical Representations of Cult*.

John F. A. Sawyer (ed.), *Reading Leviticus: A Conversation with Mary Douglas*.

Questions to Consider

1. What particular benefits do the covenantal and legal systems offer?

2. Does explication of a commandment influence, one way or another, the decision to keep it?

The "Conquest"
(Deuteronomy 20–21, 27–31; Book of Joshua)
Lecture 12

> If you read the Book of Joshua quickly ... it looks like the Book is presenting a blitzkrieg. Joshua and the Israelites get into the land, conquer Jericho, conquer the city of Ai, make it all the way through, and finally at the end, they make a covenant renewal ceremony at Shechem.. This was the greatest battle program ever enjoined. And, in fact, if we had been reading the Bible through, this is what we would have expected.

This lecture moves to the second part of the *Tanakh*, the *Nevi'im* (Prophets), with its first volume, the Book of Joshua. The Book of Deuteronomy provides the thematic framework for Joshua–2 Kings. The pattern is one known from suzerainty/vassal models: Those who follow God will prosper; those who stray will be cursed (Deut. 28:1–68). We shall discuss the laws of Deuteronomy in greater detail in Lecture 19, because the volume appears to have been implemented under King Josiah in the late 7th century. This lecture notes the details of Moses's death.

Moses is forbidden to enter Canaan (Deut. 31:2; 32:51–52). The Lord told Moses to "command a rock to bring forth water, but Moses struck the rock twice with his staff" (Num. 20:2–13; see also Exod. 17:1–7). "The Lord said to Moses and Aaron, 'Because you did not trust in me, to show my holiness before the eyes of the Israelites, therefore you shall not bring this assembly into the land that I have given them'" (Num. 20:12). Moses's final moments prepare Israel for the next stage of existence (Deut. 31). He blesses the tribes as a father would his children (Deut. 33:1–29; cf. Gen. 49). He is buried in Moab, but "no one knows his burial place to this day" (Deut. 34:6). He was 120 years old: his sight was perfect; his body, whole.

God had promised the patriarchs, Moses, and the covenant community the land "flowing with milk and honey" (Deut. 27:3), but they have to fight for it. A priest reminds the soldiers of the divine presence in battle. Officers discharge anyone who has built a new home, planted a vineyard but not enjoyed its fruit, and become engaged but not yet wed, and the faint-hearted. The ordinances enjoin against uncontrolled destruction (Deut. 20–21). The first initiative is to offer terms of peace at the price of forced labor. If surrender is denied, all adult males are to be killed, not women and children. Trees are not to be cut down. A captive woman is allowed a month's mourning period (to avoid rape). She may then become a soldier's wife; he is not permitted to sell her or to treat her as a slave. The exception to sparing lives: For a town "that the Lord your God is giving you as an inheritance, you must not let anything that breathes remain alive" (Deut. 20:16).

The Book of Joshua appears initially to be a straightforward recounting of the Israelites' "holy war" in the "promised land." The narrative impression of the "conquest" of Canaan receives archaeological support. The Hyksos, an Asiatic group, moved into Egypt in the 1720s. This could be seen to match the time when Joseph served as advisor to Pharaoh. With the rise of Egypt's Eighteenth Dynasty, c. 1570, the Hyksos were expelled. According to Exod. 12:40, "the time that the people of Israel dwelled in Egypt was 430 years"; 1720 - 1310 = 410. The Exodus Pharaoh is traditionally viewed as Ramses II, c. 1290; 1720 (Hyksos' arrival) - 1290 (Ramses II) = 430 (the number of years Exodus places the Hebrews in Egypt). This would date the conquest to the late 13th century. Archaeology attests a number of Canaanite cities destroyed in the late 1200s, including Beth-El, Debir, Lachish, Megiddo, and Hazor.

Josh. 1–11 contains several etiologies. The conquest of Ai (Josh. 7–8) is problematic: the name means "heap." Perhaps later Israelites developed the story to explain Benjaminite possession of the ruined site. The Jericho *tel* (an artificial mound of city debris) indicates consistent inhabitation from the Calcolithic (4,000–3,000 B.C.E.) through the Middle Bronze (1800–1500) Ages, but not in the Late Bronze Age (1500–1200), although the *tel* experienced severe erosion), which is the time of the conquest. Perhaps the prostitute Rahab's story is an etiology explaining Canaanite presence in the community, even as the story of Jericho explains the ruins. Josh. 10:16–27 offers an etiology of the unusually large stones blocking the entrance to the plain of Makkedah: the story of the entrapment of the five kings. Judges 1 provides a list of negative possessions—Beth She'an, Dor, Megiddo, Gezer, Acco, Sidon, and so on—indicating that occupation was at best incomplete.

A famous alternative, known as the "immigration model," has also been proposed. The immigration model is a relatively peaceful migration into the sparsely populated hill country. The tribes may represent population waves. Six "Leah tribes" (Reuben, Simeon, Levi, Judah, Isacchar, Zebulon) and four "concubine tribes" (Dan, Naphtali, Gad, Asher) settle west of the Jordan. The Rachel tribes (Ephraim, Manasseh, Benjamin) arrive with Yahwism (cf. exhortations to "put away the gods which your ancestors served beyond the river and in Egypt and serve the Lord" [Josh. 24:14]). Simeon and Levi settle in the central hills but scatter under pressure from nearby Shechem (cf. Gen. 34, 49). Judah annexes Simeon, and Levi loses its land grant. Both tribes are absent from the Song of Deborah (Jdg. 5). Fragments of Reuben are absorbed into Judah and Gad; Reuben's relations with Bilhah, Jacob's concubine, provide the etiology for tribal disintegration.

The Amarna Letters hint of a peaceful process of resettlement in Canaan by outsiders (including the Apiru). Issachar's area, including Shunem and Mt. Tabor, is cited in the Amarna Letters about Megiddo's king, who forced people from Shunem to act as slave-porters. Gen. 49:15 says of Issachar: "He saw that the resting place was good and that the land was pleasant, so he bowed his shoulder to bear and became a slave at forced labor." Perhaps Issachar acquired its territory by serving for it; the tribe's name can be translated "worker for wages."

The immigration model also explains mysterious references to the Tribe of Dan. Josh. 19:40–48 connects Dan with Philistine settlements on the Mediterranean. Jdg. 5:17, the Song of Deborah, asks why Dan "lingered by the ships." Gen. 49:16: "Dan shall judge his people as one of the tribes of Israel"; an odd statement, unless Dan is originally alien. Is this a connection to a group of sea peoples called the Denyen, Danaoi, and/or Danuna?

Other tribes may also carry non-Hebrew pedigrees. Asher from Assur (the Assyrian god) or Asherah (the Canaanite goddess). Gad is a Canaanite god.

Zebulun, which means "of the princes," is an epithet of the Canaanite Baal. The covenant-making ceremony at Shechem (Josh. 24) raises historical problems. Joshua mentions the Exodus and the wilderness and invokes Abraham, Isaac, Jacob, Esau, Moses, and Aaron but omits reference to the Sinaitic covenant. Perhaps the Exodus experience represents the collective memory of one group and the Sinaitic theophany, the experience of another. Shechem may have been occupied by Hebrews before the "conquest" (cf. Gen. 34), and the Amarna Letters locate Apiru in Shechem.

Prompted in part by studies in social revolution, some scholars—sparked by the work of George Mendenhall—posit a revolt by an indigenous population. To avoid oligarchies, the revolutionaries made the struggle for power an illicit assumption of divine prerogatives. Yahwism provided the catalyst for this new organization and ideology. Because the removal of kings was done by indigenous groups, no major military action was involved and, thus, no major story recorded.

The so-called "conquest" is likely a composite story of internal and external groups motivated by various political, religious, economic, and ideological concerns. They eventually established common cause and, later, common history. The Book of Joshua, joining history and folktale, represents a point toward the end of that process, when the traditions were becoming harmonized. One might view Joshua as part of a Hexateuch, a six-scroll collection, which completes the patriarchal promise. The Book of Judges, to which we turn next, offers testimony to the role of independent tribal units, even as it anticipates the creation of the monarchy. ■

Suggested Reading

Susan Niditch, *War in the Hebrew Bible: A Study in the Ethics of Violence.*

Questions to Consider

1. Is holy war simply "wholly war," or is it ever justified? If the latter, and based on what you have read in the Bible to this point, does the Book of Joshua describe such an occasion?

2. Is Rahab a hero, a traitor, or a self-serving survivor?

3. According to Deut. 31:10, "Never since has there arisen a prophet in Israel like Moses, whom the Lord knew face to face." Is it appropriate that he be denied entry into the promised land? That he have no memorial or tomb (compared, for example, to the patriarchs and matriarchs at Hebron; Rachel's tomb)?

The Book of Judges, Part I
(Judges 1–8)
Lecture 13

> Gone is the time of miracles, the sun standing still, or the trumpets blaring and the walls of Jericho falling. In fact, gone is the time when you can tell the difference between the good guys and the bad guys. When we move to the Book of Judges, it is as if we are coming closer to our own world.

The Book of Judges is, as Mieke Bal describes, "a book about death." Repeating the type scene of apostasy, punishment, repentance, and rescue, the book ultimately spirals into idolatry, rape, and near-genocide. Yet the barbarity is broken by moments of delight. Judges plays on traditional definitions of the hero: tricksters like Ehud, mothers like Deborah, cowards like Gideon, tragic figures like Jephthah, even blockheads like Samson. Offering high comedy and profound tragedy, Judges continues to raise historical, theological, and moral challenges.

Judges is set c. 1200–1000, at the beginning of the Iron Age. The narrative suggests a long editorial process culminating shortly before or during Babylonian captivity in the 6th century. Individual tribal legends are combined in the Deuteronomic editorial framework: the view that fidelity is rewarded and apostasy punished. The type scene guides all but the last several chapters. The basic pattern appears with the first judge, Othniel, in 3:7–11: "The people of Israel did what was evil" (3:7). YHWH gives them to Cushan-Rishathaim of Mesopotamia for eight years (3:8). The people cry out to the Lord, and "the Lord raised up a deliverer for the people of Israel" (3:9). Othniel receives the divine spirit, wages war, and prevails (3:10). Othniel judges Israel forty years, then dies (3:11), "and the people of Israel again did what was evil" (3:12). Even this introductory pattern is broken by textual anecdotes. Othniel is less stalwart than his betrothed, Caleb's daughter Acsah. Acsah and Caleb function as ironic foils to Jephthah and his daughter (Jdg. 11).

The first variation, the account of Ehud, is so sexual and scatological that it was just as likely a favorite of ancient Israel even as it is rarely cited from pulpits and bimas today. Ehud the trickster prevails by means of brains, not brawn. Like cross-cultural tricksters (Pan, Loki, Hermes), he is left-handed. This trait allows him to conceal his weapon: he "girded [the sword] on his right thigh under his clothes" (Jdg. 3:16). A sexual undertone begins.

King Eglon, the enemy, also possesses an unusual characteristic: he is "very fat" (3:17). Because kings are military leaders, Eglon is already shown to be unworthy. That *eglon* means "fatted calf" hints that he will be sacrificed to that hidden sword.

The judge's victory is filled with sexual and scatological imagery common to folktales. Ehud states (3:19), "I have a message for you, O king," and the king, stupidly, orders everyone except Ehud away. "Ehud came to him, as [Eglon] was sitting alone in his cool roof chamber" (3:20). "Ehud reached with his left hand" (the hand used for handling genitals; 3:21). He "took his sword from his right thigh, and thrust it into Eglon's belly ... the hilt went in after the blade, and the fat closed over the blade." The image is of perverse intercourse. Reading 3:22 euphemistically: "And the dirt came out"; more directly, the king defecates—there is an emission, but the wrong kind. Eglon's servants, believing that the king is relieving himself, avoid entering and, thus, permit Ehud to escape. "They waited until they were utterly at a loss; but when he still did not open the doors of the roof chamber, they took the key and opened them, and there lay their lord, dead on the floor" (3:25). Shamgar is the next judge, though little is said of him. He provides a break between the account of Ehud and the Song of Deborah.

The story of Deborah (Jdg. 4–5), told first in prose, then in poetry, plays on the themes of mothers, violence, and seduction. Deborah's introduction challenges military, gendered, and maternal conventions. Underneath her palm tree, the judge presides before the military problems arise. Most translations render 4:1 "wife of Lappidoth," but no such character appears. The phrase could be translated "woman of flames," which complements the name of her general, Barak ("lightning"). Her relationship to Barak complicates gender roles. Barak refuses initially to battle: "If you go with me,

I will go; but if you will not go with me, I will not go" (4:8). This passage may be read, however, as Barak's testing of Deborah. Deborah agrees, but at the price of his honor: "The road on which you are going will not lead to your glory, for the Lord will sell [the enemy] Sisera into the hand of a woman" (4:9).

The "woman" who claims the honor Barak loses is Jael, the second "mother." Jael is married to the absent but frequently mentioned "Heber the Kenite [who] had separated from the Kenites, the descendants of Hobab the father-in-law of Moses." (In the next lecture, we shall see how far Moses's household has fallen.) Sisera, the enemy general, fleeing Barak, goes "to the tent of Jael, the wife of Heber the Kenite, for there was peace between Jabin the King of Hazor and the house of Heber the Kenite." But what of Jael: Is she Israelite, Kenite, Canaanite? To whom are her loyalties? Are we to be reminded of Cain: a murderer, yet protected?

Deborah, the only female judge.

Jael inverts Near Eastern concerns for hospitality and conventions of motherhood. Her invitation is more seduction than protection: "Jael came out to meet Sisera, and said to him, 'Turn aside, my lord, turn aside to me; have no fear'" (4:18). Maternally: "She covered him with a rug. And he said to her, 'Pray, give me a little water to drink, for I am thirsty.' So she opened a skin of milk and gave him a drink and covered him" (4:19). Then "the wife of Heber, took a tent peg, and went softly to him, and drove the peg into his temple, until it went down into the ground, as he was lying fast asleep from weariness. So he died." The imagery evokes Eglon's death: sword and tent peg, trickster assassins, bedroom demise.

The Song of Deborah offers one of the oldest examples of Hebrew poetry. The song restages Sisera's death: he is standing as he dies, and his unmanning becomes even more manifest:

> She struck Sisera a blow
>
> She crushed his head
>
> She shattered and pierced his temple.
>
> He sank, he fell.
>
> He lay still at her feet.
>
> At her feet he sank, he fell;
>
> Where he sank, there he fell, done to death.

The song also mentions a third mother. Unlike Deborah and Jael, Sisera's mother is inside a home, not under a tree or in a tent; she has all the luxuries of the city-state, yet she lacks peace:

> Out of the window she peered.
>
> The mother of Sisera gazed through the lattice.
>
> Why is his chariot so long in coming?
>
> Why tarry the hoofbeats of his chariots?

Before Deborah's song allows too much sympathy, Sisera's mother develops her own explanation.

> Are they not finding and dividing the spoil?
>
> A womb or two or every man?
>
> Spoil of dyed stuff for Sisera ... ?
>
> She will receive neither.

Gideon's story (Judges 6–8) reveals increasing problems with charismatic leaders who are less confident and less capable. The convention expands description of the judge's appointment: In the modern idiom, "good men are becoming harder to find." Gideon complains about the weakness of his tribe (Manasseh), family, and personal ability. He also complains about divine inaction. As Gideon is beating wheat in the winepress to hide it from the Midianites, an angel announces, "The Lord is with you, you mighty man of valor" (6:11). Given Gideon's position, the sarcasm is palpable. Gideon responds: "Pray sir, if the Lord is with us, why then has all this befallen us? And where are all his wonderful deeds, which our ancestors recounted to us, saying, 'Did not the Lord bring us up out of Egypt?'" Gideon risks trivializing divine ability by continually testing God. He taxes God's patience—and the reader's: "Let not your anger burn against me; let me speak but this once. Pray, let me make trial only this once with the fleece; pray let it be dry only this once on the fleece, and on all the ground let there be dew" (6:39).

This unpromising beginning matches his unpromising end. Gideon's other name is "Jerubaal," "Let Baal contend," a Canaanite "Israel." His final action, one of apostasy, confirms his fall: "Gideon made an ephod of [the gold captured from the Midianites] and put it in his city in Ophrah; all Israel whored after it there, and it became a snare to Gideon and his family" (8:27).

One of his sons, Abimelech ("my father is king"), will prove to be a false judge. With his tenure, the benefits of the charismatic leader become increasingly insecure. As we shall see in the next lecture, the role of the judge must eventually cede to that of the king. ∎

Suggested Reading

Susan Ackerman, *Warrior, Dancer, Seductress, Queen: Women in Judges and Biblical Israel*, Anchor Bible Reference Library.

Mieke Bal, *Death and Dissymmetry: The Politics of Coherence in the Book of Judges*.

Gail Yee (ed.), *Judges and Method: New Approaches in Biblical Studies*.

Questions to Consider

1. Is Judges "funny"?

2. What are the functions of such motifs as scatology, perverse sexual humor, and reversed gender roles (military women, mothers who kill, generals who seek protection from women) in a community's national epic?

3. What is the "theology" of Judges?

The Book of Judges, Part II
(Judges 8–21)
Lecture 14

> A judge is not simply someone who would sit in a courtroom and engage in decision making over land disputations or over whose ox gored whose. To the contrary, judges are charismatic leaders imbued by the spirit of God. ... In the second part of the Book of Judges, that the entire institution begins to break down as the judges don't immediately receive the spirit or don't receive it at all as they make rash vows, and, by the time we get up to Samson, they are not even aware of what their divine commission is.

Abimelech, the false judge, embodies the threat of dynasties. His usurpation of power highlights the inevitable dynastic problem: competition. Gideon rejected dynastic rule (8:22–23) in favor of rule by God. Abimelech, the child of Gideon's Shechemite concubine, convinces the Shechemites that he, rather than one of the seventy sons of Gideon's wives, would make their appropriate leader: nepotism triumphs over legitimacy and qualification. Abimelech kills all his seventy brothers save Jotham, the youngest (9:5). Throughout the Deuteronomic history, dynastic succession exists in tension with the traditions of charismatic leaders and the ambivalence concerning primogeniture. Although Gideon consistently receives divine aid, God sends an "evil spirit" between Abimelech and the Shechemite lords (9:23); rulers require divine as well as political support. Abimelech exacerbates his father's idolatry. Gideon (Jerubaal) made an *ephod*, likely an image of a local god (8:27). Abimelech, supported by his Shechemite mother's relatives, receives funding from the Shechemite temple of "*Ba'al Berit*" (ironically, "Lord of the Covenant" [9:4]). The scene evokes Gen. 34, the rape of Jacob's daughter by Shechem (the prince of the land and, symbolically, the entire city). Abimelech is killed when "some woman" (9:53) drops a millstone on his head. Horrified at this ignoble end, Abimelech orders his aide to kill him (9:50–57). The scene ends not with a reigning judge and peace, but a dead judge and a curse.

Jephthah (11:1–12:7), the tragic judge, shows the problems with appropriate selection. "Jephthah ... the son of a prostitute, was a mighty warrior ... When [Gilead's] wife's sons grew up, they drove Jephthah away, saying to him, 'You shall not inherit anything in our father's house, for you are the son of another woman'" (11:1–2). The opening recollects Ishmael and Isaac (Gen. 21:10). It anticipates David: Both rulers function initially as outlaws (Jdg. 11:3; 1 Sam. 25).

Jephthah is commissioned not by God, but by his town's leaders: "Are you not the very ones who rejected me and drove me out of my father's house?" Yet he agrees: "*If you bring me home again* ... I will be your head" (11:9). The reversal of the convention and the absence of divine involvement indicate the breakdown of the political system. The conditional response anticipates the rash vow Jephthah later makes. The desire for "home" increases Jephthah's tragedy.

Later (11:29), "the spirit of the Lord" comes upon Jephthah. He immediately vows: "If you will give the Ammonites into my hand, then whoever comes out of the doors of my house to meet me, when I return victorious from the Ammonites, shall be the Lord's, to be offered up by me as a burnt offering" (11:30–31). The lateness of the commission raises questions of divine culpability. The vow has no excuse. Jephthah appears incapable of accepting his own worth.

At the victory, Jephthah's daughter emerges—as is typical for women—in celebration: "She was his only child. He had no son or daughter except her" (11:34). The verse echoes the *Akedah*: "your son, your only son ..." Jephthah blames his daughter: "Alas, my daughter, you have brought me very low. You have become the cause of great trouble to me ..." (11:35). She supports him: "My father, you have opened your mouth to the Lord; do to me according to what has gone forth from your mouth ..." The sacrifice is delayed while the daughter mourns her virginity. This becomes "a custom in Israel," perhaps a puberty or premarital rite. Or, as J. Cheryl Exum suggests, is "she" "an example" of daughters sacrificed to fathers' interests (cf. Othniel and Acsah; later, Saul and Michal)?

Jephthah's victory comes at the expense of tribal unity when Ephraim revolts. The problem is now internal to Israel, not external. His household tragedy assumes national implications.

Samson, Israel's Hercules (13:1–16:31), will eclipse, like the sun that is his leitmotif. Samson's nativity spoofs conventional annunciations. His parents are childless, and there is no indication that they want children, unlike their Genesis counterparts. Mrs. Manoah meets an angel in the field who announces, "Behold, you are barren and have no child." This is news? The angel informs Mrs. Manoah that she will become pregnant, the child should be a Nazirite, and he will deliver his people from the Philistines. She accepts this oracle without question; the same cannot be said for Manoah (13:6). Manoah, after a ridiculous conversation with the angel, invites the angel to lunch (cf. Gen. 18:1–15); the angel suggests offering

Samson and Delilah.

a sacrifice instead, which he does. When the angel ascends in the flames, Manoah fears he and his wife will die, because they have "seen God." His wife retorts, "If the Lord had meant to kill us, he would not have accepted the burnt offering ..." (13:23).

Samson's career spoofs, then tragically reverses, that of other judges. Breaking his Nazirite vows, Samson consumes honey from a lion's carcass. He thus violates the commandment against eating (from) carrion. He insists on marrying a Philistine, against his parents' objections. When Samson is betrayed by his wife, his "military" action is against his bride's family. Samson burns Philistine fields; the Philistines burn Samson's wife and her father.

Delilah, the woman "from Sorek" whom Samson loved, is a complex figure. Viewed as Philistine, Delilah has a Hebrew name (cognate to *Layla*, "night"); she is the inverse of Samson, the symbol of sun and fire. Viewed as immoral, she never lies to Samson, but she does betray him to the Philistines. Viewed as mercenary, her motives are unexpressed: Might she fear Philistine reprisal? Is her cajoling a warning?

The story can be read at its end as if it is a tragedy like the story of Oedipus. Why does Samson reveal his secret to Delilah? She arranges to have his hair, the source of his power, shaved off. Returned to a state of infancy—bald, sightless, and helpless—Samson eventually regains hair, strength, and a modicum of maturity. He dies pulling down the Philistine temple. Thus ends the period of the judges.

With the Danites, the type scene is fully broken; chaos follows. Micah's story hints of Samson's and anticipates that of the Levite's concubine. Micah is "in the hill country of Ephraim," the Levite's home (17:1; 19:1). He obtains from his mother the "cursed" eleven hundred pieces of silver (17:1), the same amount received for Samson's betrayal. He buys a Levite and procures Teraphim, but the Danites steal both. The Danites represent the descent of the community into apostasy (18:1–31). Jonathan, son of Gershom, son of Moses (some manuscripts read "Manasseh"), and his sons were priests to the Danites until the exile. Dan and Beth-el held the Northern Kingdom's major shrines: perhaps this story and the next developed c. 622, during Josiah's reform, which included disenfranchising Levites and centralizing sacrifice in Jerusalem. The story is prefaced by "In those days there was no king in Israel" (18:1).

The story of the Levite's concubine reprises Sodom's destruction (Gen. 19), without divine intervention. The narrative opens with a text-critical problem. The Septuagint (19:2) reads that the concubine "became angry with [the

Levite]." The Hebrew reads, "she played the whore" (anticipating prophetic metaphors). The Levite follows her "to speak tenderly to her" (19:3). The expression recollects Shechem, Dinah's rapist, and, again, anticipates prophetic metaphors.

The story replaces Sodom with a Benjaminite city. The Levite bypasses lodging in the non-Israelite city, Jebus; this is Jerusalem. When they enter Gibeah, another Ephraimite gives them lodging. The Benjaminites, "a perverse lot," demand of the stranger, "that we may know him." The old man, like Lot, offers his own virgin daughter and Levite's concubine. The Levite "seized his concubine and put her out to them. They wantonly raped her, and abused her all the night until the morning" (19:25). In the morning, the Levite, seeing her "lying at the door of the house, with her hands on the threshold," commands: "Get up; we are going" (19:27–28). "She made no reply." The concubine's body now summons, and symbolizes, broken Israel. The Levite, in a perverse sacrifice, hacks her body into twelve pieces, which he distributes to the tribes. The attendant message is: "Has such a thing ever happened since the day that the Israelites came up from the land of Egypt?" (19:30). The tribes gather; the war leads to more loss as Benjamin's existence is threatened. To preserve the tribe, hundreds of women are given to Benjamin; rapes escalate. The text ends with the refrain "there was no king in Israel; every man did what was right in his own eyes" (21:25), and so sets the stage for the monarchy. ■

Suggested Reading

Phyllis Trible, *Texts of Terror: Literary-Feminist Readings of Biblical Narratives*.

See also works listed for Lecture 13.

Questions to Consider

1. Does the sacrifice of Jephthah's daughter provoke a reconsideration of the *Akedah*?

2. Why does Delilah, along with other women who trick men (such as Potiphar's wife in Gen. 39, a story we have not directly addressed) escape narrative judgment?

3. How does the story of Moses from Exodus through Deuteronomy contribute both to supporting the institution of the charismatic leader and undermining this system in favor of a dynastic monarchy?

Samuel and Saul
(1 Samuel)
Lecture 15

First Samuel does not begin with a monarchy. To the contrary, it begins with the birth of Samuel and what looks like a very calm and pleasant society, as if somehow we're back to the good old days.

The tribal confederacy under the leadership of judges had disintegrated, but the increasing threat of Philistine power made a centralized government desirable. Samuel, who represents the transition from charismatic leader to prophet, combines the roles of priest, prophet, and judge. His wife's personal emptiness symbolizes the problems of the nation. Unable to have a child, Hannah recollects Sarah, Rebecca, and Rachel. Mocked by her fertile co-wife, she resembles Sarah. So distressed about her infertility, when her husband asks, "Am I not more to you than ten sons?" (1 Sam. 1:8), she can make no answer.

At Shiloh, her encounter with the priest Eli anticipates the fall of Eli's house and implies the rejection of the priest as national leader at this stage of Israel's history. Hannah prays passionately for a child; Eli, seeing her lips move but hearing no words, assumes she is drunk and berates her. Eli cannot control his sons, who take the best portions of the sacrifices (1 Sam. 2:12–17) and have intercourse with women at the sanctuary (2:22). When Hannah relates the truth, Eli prophesies her pregnancy and, thereby, evokes the annunciation type scene. She promises to dedicate her son to God; he will, therefore, replace Eli's sons.

Hannah's hymn, "The Song of Hannah" (the model for Mary's Magnificat [Luke 1:46–55]), introduces extensive political concerns. It predicts social upheaval: the mighty brought down; the weak uplifted. It predicts Hannah's own changing circumstance: the barren made fertile. It locates the monarchy under divine support and direction.

Samuel's commission comes while he is under Eli's care. Weaning Samuel, Hannah brings him to Shiloh; each year, she returns, bringing him a knitted coat (2:19). The "word of the Lord" (3:1), "rare in those days," comes to Samuel when he is "lying down in the temple, where the ark of God was" (3:3). Eli's promise of a dynasty, offered in 2:30, is revoked, and Samuel becomes God's agent: "All Israel from Dan to Beersheva knew that Samuel was established as a prophet of the Lord ... for the Lord revealed himself to Samuel at Shiloh ..." (3:19–4:1). Samuel combines the strengths of Israel's earlier leaders: Like Moses, God speaks to him; like Aaron, he has priestly duties; like Joshua, he unites the people and sets up a witness-stone (called "Ebenezer," stone of help, 7:12), like Deborah, he "judged Israel all the days of his life" (7:15).

That Samuel and his role as judge, prophet, and priest will not prevail is foreshadowed by the capture of the ark, the first event to occur under his leadership (1 Sam. 4–7). The ark's peripatetic journey adds unexpected humor. When the ark is brought to the Philistine temple at Ashdod, Dagon the idol keeps bowing to it. Re-erected, the idol falls apart. Ashdod's residents ship the ark to Gath, the home of Goliath. Breaking out in "tumors" (RSV) or "hemorrhoids" (JB), the Gathites ship the ark to Ekron. The people of Ekron cry, "They have brought around to us the ark of the God of Israel, to slay us and our people" (5:10). Finally, the Philistines tie the ark to two cows, which head to Beth Shemesh. There, the Levites detach the ark and sacrifice the cows. The ark remains in Keriath-Je'arim for twenty years, until David establishes his capital in Jerusalem (2 Sam. 6).

Samuel's history frames the ark narrative: It begins when he takes office; it ends with a mention of his latter years. "When Samuel became old, he made his sons judges over Israel ... his sons did not walk in his ways, but turned aside after gain; they took bribes and perverted justice" (1 Sam. 8:1–3). The "unworthy son" motif (Moses, Gideon, Eli) continues the polemic against dynastic succession. Given that the judge, priest, and prophet cannot establish permanent leadership, government must derive from a new source.

We see arguments both for and against kingship in 1 Samuel 8–11. The people want a king "to govern us like all the nations" (8:5). Their request undermines YHWH's kingship and compromises the tradition's egalitarian impulse. Samuel notes: kings take sons to populate armies; daughters, for the palace staff. "He will take a tenth of your flocks ..." "And you shall be his slaves" (8:17). 1 Samuel 9 offers a pro-monarchical perspective. Samuel appears not as the national prophet but as a local "seer." The Deity appears to favor not a king, but a prince: "I will send you a man from Benjamin, and you shall anoint him to be a prince over my people Israel." The impetus is practical: "He shall save my people from ... the Philistines" (9:16–17).

Ambivalence about kingship is complemented by ambivalence about Saul. His introduction implies that his qualifications are looks and wealth. "There was a man of Benjamin whose name was Kish ... a man of wealth. And he had a son whose name was Saul, a handsome young man. There was not a man among the people of Israel more handsome than he; from his shoulders upward he was taller than any of his people" (9:1–2). Saul's first action is his failure to fulfill a type scene. He "meets young maidens coming out to draw water" (9:11), but his mind is set on finding Kish's lost donkeys. He finds, not donkeys, but royal anointing. Like Moses and Gideon, Saul is a reluctant leader; he is also reluctantly anointed. He is only "a Benjaminite, from the least of the tribes of Israel: "And is not my family the humblest of all the families of the tribes of Benjamin?" (9:21). Samuel first anoints Saul in secret, as if God only minimally accedes to the people's demand. When Samuel makes a public announcement, the process makes the choice of Saul anticlimactic: Lots are cast to see whom God will choose for the king. The lots fall on Saul, but "when they sought him he could not be found. So they inquired again of the Lord ... and the Lord said, 'Behold, he has hidden himself among the baggage'" (10:22). Samuel asserts: "Do you see him whom the Lord has chosen? There is none like him among all the people."

As Israel struggles to harmonize traditional egalitarianism with a centralized monarch, Saul also has difficulty negotiating his role. Samuel may have plotted his failure, "Samuel did not come to Gilgal, and the people were scattering. So Saul said, 'Bring the burnt offerings here to me, and the peace offerings'" (13:8–9). The king usurps the priestly role. As Saul completes the sacrifice, Samuel arrives to pronounce condemnation: "Your kingdom shall not continue" (13:14). Instead of sacrificing the spoils of the Amalekite raid, "Saul and the people spared Agag [the king], and the best of the sheep and the oxen and the fatlings, and the lambs, and all that was good, and would not utterly destroy them" (15:9). God "repents" of making Saul king. Condemned by Samuel, Saul repents, but too late: "Samuel hewed Agag to pieces before the Lord at Gilgal" (15:33). "Samuel did not see Saul again until the day of his death" (15:35).

The death of Agag.

Saul's untenable political position culminates in his final tragedy. Suffering when the "evil spirit from God" (16:23) overtakes him, Saul is comforted only by his harp player. His torment is divinely caused. His harp player will usurp his throne. Saul's son and daughter will betray him. His death confirms the fragility of his rule. Facing Philistine onslaught, Saul finds himself needing Samuel's advice. Yet Samuel is dead, and "Saul had put the mediums and wizards out of the land" (28:3). Saul, contravening his own law, seeks a medium. Attesting to the ineffectuality of Saul's national policies, his soldiers quickly find one in Endor.

The medium tells Saul, "I see a god coming up out of the earth" (28:13). When he inquires about its appearance, she responds: "An old man is coming up, and he is wrapped in a cloak." The term matches that used for the coats Hannah had made, and Saul knew that the man was Samuel. Told by Samuel that he will lose the battle, the king refuses to eat; the medium—whose livelihood and life were threatened by Saul's policies—feeds him dinner. The next morning, Saul and his son Jonathan die in battle. Making lament for them is their rival, the next king, David, to whose story we turn in the next lecture. ■

Suggested Reading

David Jobling, *First Samuel*.

Questions to Consider

1. Why is Saul made a sympathetic character?

2. Considering the previous seven biblical books, what model of political leadership would appear most beneficial for Israel?

3. What is compromised in the egalitarian (if androcentric) nature of Israelite religion, under the covenant, by the monarchy?

Note: The Book of Ruth appears between Judges and 1 Samuel in Christian canons. Both because most scholars date the book's composition to a period later than these texts and because in the MT, it appears in the *Ketuvim* (Writings), discussion of Ruth is reserved for a later lecture.

King David
(1 Samuel 16–31, 2 Samuel, 1 Kings 1–2)
Lecture 16

David's accession anticipates a period of tribal unification, prosperity, and peace with neighboring kingdoms; the royal grant by which the Deity adopts David and guarantees that his descendants will hold the throne of Israel in perpetuity (1 Sam. 7) appears to confirm his promise. However, David's own failures lead to familial strife, civil war, and the bloody route to Solomon's throne.

The story of David is worthy of an entire course. His story encompasses myriad roles, including the erstwhile shepherd whose music soothes King Saul's spirit (1 Sam. 16); the armor-bearer whose shot kills the Philistine champion Goliath (1 Sam. 17); the enemy of Saul, but the intimate of Saul's son Jonathan and husband to Saul's daughter Michal (1 Sam. 18 *passim*); the leader of a gang of malcontents and the Philistine vassal (1 Sam. 22–27); the king granted an eternal covenant (2 Sam. 7); the adulterer who arranges the death of his lover's husband (2 Sam. 12); the father whose beloved son, Absalom, wars against him (2 Sam. 13–20); and the old man who cannot find warmth (1 Kings 1). David can be viewed as a culture hero, similar to King Arthur. David's history receives no uncontested support from external

King David playing the lyre.

evidence. An inscription possibly reading "house of David" has been found among fragments of Iron Age pottery. Some archaeologists claim that the inscription testifies to David's existence; others question both its date and its age. The attribution to him of Goliath's death may be an example of form criticism at work: The story remains the same, but the characters change. Second Sam. 21:19 attributes Goliath's death to David's soldier, Elhanan.

The opening verses signal political and personal deficiencies; David's domestic failures foreshadow and serve as a microcosm of the ensuing civil war. "In the spring of the year, the time when kings go out to battle, David sent Joab with his officers and all Israel with him, and they ravaged the Ammonites ... but David remained in Jerusalem." Clearly, he was not attending to his duties. "It happened, late one afternoon, when David rose from his couch and was walking about on the roof of the king's house, that he saw from the roof a woman bathing; the woman was very beautiful." Is this David, described as "skilled in music, a man of valor and a warrior, sensible in speech and handsome in appearance, and the lord is with him" (1 Sam. 16:18)?

Interpreters question Bathsheba's complicity in David's downfall. Does she see him as he sees her? Had she planned to be seen? Does she know the king's movements?

David's relationship with Bathsheba is premeditated: "David sent for messengers and inquired and said, 'Isn't this Bathsheba ... the wife of Uriah the Hittite?" The scene recollects David's other relationships, including: His marriage to the clever Abigail, after complicity in causing her first husband's death (1 Sam. 16:1–25). His marriage to Michal, who loves, then despises him, and "who had no child to the day of her death" (2 Sam. 23).

Whether David can "love" is an open question. Jonathan loves David, to such an extent that he, Saul's son and heir, betrays his own father and king. David makes public lament over the prince's dead body: "I am distressed for you, my brother Jonathan/greatly beloved were you to me. Your love to me was wonderful/passing the love of women" (2 Sam. 1:26). David even orders the song to be "taught to the people of Judah" (2 Sam.1:18). But David does not say he *loved* Jonathan. The more cynical reader would see the lament as opportunistic.

"So David sent messengers to get her, and she came to him and he lay with her. (Now she was purifying herself after her period)" (2 Sam. 11:4). Did David abuse his power? Had Bathsheba a choice when the "messengers" arrived? Is this rape? Is this the "romance" of popular legend? Had David read Deut. 22:22 on the punishment for adultery? And what of Bathsheba? Is this the fulfillment of her plans? Why does the text explicitly note that "she came to him"? Is she depicted as faithful in her ritual practices, or simply as not pregnant?

"The woman conceived, and she sent and told David, 'I am pregnant'" (11:5). David is the father, because Bathsheba was introduced as purifying herself at the completion of her menstrual cycle. What does Bathsheba want David to do with this information? First, the coveting of the neighbor's wife, then adultery, then murder? David recalls Uriah and encourages him to "go down to your house and wash your feet." This is an invitation to connubiality, because "feet"—Hebrew: *reglayim*—is a euphemism for genitalia. Uriah refuses: "The ark and Israel and Judah remain in booths ... shall I then go to my house, to eat and to drink and to lie with my wife? As you live, and as your soul lives, I shall not do such a thing." David even gets Uriah drunk, but still he demurs. Finally, David sends him back with a sealed letter to Joab: Place Uriah "in the forefront of the hardest fighting, and then draw back from him, so that he may be struck down and die" (2 Sam. 11:15).

Bathsheba—after a time of mourning—marries David and bears a son. But "the thing David had done displeased the Lord" (11:27). Initially, it is not clear what the "thing" is: Rape? Adultery? Uriah's murder? Marriage to Bathsheba? Sinning against God? How can one atone for voyeurism, adultery, murder, and cover-up? oes David recognize his protection under the royal grant? God speaks to David through Nathan: "You have struck down Uriah the Hittite with the sword, and have taken his wife to be your wife... now therefore the sword shall never depart from your house ... I will take your wives from before your eyes, and give them to your neighbor, and he shall lie with your wives in the sight of this very sun. For you did it secretly, but I will do this before all Israel" (2 Sam. 12: 10-12). Adultery is never private: It involves messengers, coworkers, confidants. It affects even one's children: Amnon rapes Tamar, and Absalom—leading a civil war against his father—will rape David's concubines on the palace rooftop.

David admits his sin, and Nathan tells him that his sin has been passed over … at least in God's purview. Psalm 51 is titled "A Psalm of David, when the prophet Nathan came to him after he had gone in to Bathsheba." Despite David's repenting, Nathan predicts, "the child that is born to you shall die" (12:14). David and Bathsheba have a second child who, with the machinations of his mother and the prophet, obtains the throne. His name is Solomon. ■

Suggested Reading

J. Cheryl Exum, *Fragmented Women: Feminist Subversions of Biblical Narratives*.

Stephen L. McKenzie, *King David: A Biography*.

Marti J. Steussy, *David: Biblical Portraits of Power*.

Questions to Consider

1. How might the story of David function as later propaganda for the monarchy?

2. Should rulers' personal lives enter the assessment of their governing capabilities?

3. Is David admirable despite his (major) failings? If so, how? If not, what does one make of the royal grant?

From King Solomon to Preclassical Prophecy (1 Kings 3–2 Kings 17)
Lecture 17

According to the biblical tradition, Solomon was a spectacular king. ... His court becomes a center of wisdom and learning. Solomon is so wise that the biblical tradition attributes to him wisdom literature.

The biblical prophet (*Nabi*; plural: *Nevi'im*) is known less for predicting the future than for communicating divine will, usually through poetry, and often in debate with kings and priests. Prophecy thus can be separated neither from politics nor from the concern for social justice. Although Abraham, Aaron, Moses, and Miriam are all called "prophets," biblical scholarship traditionally speaks of the formal role of the prophet as beginning with the monarchy and gradually ending with the rise of the theocratic state. Let's begin with Solomon to establish a picture of the type of king against which the prophets inveighed.

The golden age of ancient Israel began with King Solomon.

Solomon becomes an ideal, and quite typical, Near Eastern king; thus, he fulfills both the pro- and anti-monarchical views expressed by Samuel. On the positive side Solomon solidifies David's political basis and geographical holdings, builds the Jerusalem Temple, establishes enormous treasury reserves, and develops a positive international reputation, as witnessed by the Queen of Sheba's embassy (1 Kings 10). His court becomes known as a center of learning, such that much of Israelite wisdom literature (the Song of Songs, Proverbs, Ecclesiastes) is attributed to him.

Thus, 1 Kings 4:29: "God gave Solomon wisdom and understanding beyond measure, and largeness of mind like the sand on the seashore."

However, on the negative side Solomon's rule is marked by *corvées* (the extrication of unpaid labor from the population). He creates an overextended economy marked by the importation of luxury items, consequently has a heavily taxed peasantry; the "golden age" of Solomon was likely golden only for the elite. Solomon also disobeys Deut. 17:14–20 concerning not only the build-up of capital, but also: "he must not acquire many wives for himself, or else his heart will turn away." "Solomon has three-hundred wives and seven-hundred concubines," who "lead his heart astray" after idols (1 Kings 11:1–8).

The temple of Solomon.

The inflated government, in conflict with the Yahwistic premise of social egalitarianism, could not survive and we see the end of a centralized government. Under Solomon's heir, Rehoboam, the northern tribes secede. David's kingdom will remain divided—Israel in the North; Judah in the South—for the next two hundred years. Israel, lacking the Davidic grant and always in a precarious situation with leaders, develops a strong counter to the power of the king: the prophet.

Let's look at divine/human communication. The Urim and Thummim, interpreted by the priests, were likely forms of lots. The King James Version of 1 Sam. 28:8 reads, "Divine for me by a familiar." The Hebrew reads *ob*, the Hittite/Akkadian cognate to which is "hole in the ground." Necromancy, consulting the dead, involves pouring wine or oil into a hole in the ground, although, because of a translation error, it has been misunderstood. Astrology is indicated in Isa. 47:13: "those who 'divide' [the meaning of the Hebrew here is uncertain] the heavens, who gaze at the stars, who at the new moons predict what will befall you." Hepatoscopy, the reading of liver omens, is the best-attested Near Eastern divinatory practice. Archaeologists have located clay livers from Hazor. The technique is noted in Ezek. 21:21: "The King of Babylon stands at the parting of the way, at the head of the two ways to use divination. He shakes the arrows, he consults the teraphim, he looks at the liver."

The division of functions. One theory argues that the office of prophet in its uniquely Hebrew sense was born when the office of judge—with its theological and gubernatorial elements—evolved into two distinct branches: prophets and kings.

An alternative, and complementary, view relates prophesy to ecstatic possession. Etymology of the Hebrew *nabi* has no clear ancient Near Eastern cognates. Its closest linguistic relation, the same root with different vowels, means "to rave like one insane" (cf. 1 Sam. 18:10, on Saul who "raved"). Prophetic ecstasy (literally, "to stand outside, or be beside, oneself") involves possession and, sometimes, an accompanying message.

Ecstatic prophecy is particularly, and problematically, associated with King Saul. Saul meets a band of prophets "coming down from the high place with harp, tambourine, lyre, and flute before them, prophesying." He is told: "The spirit of the Lord will come mightily upon you, and you shall prophecy with them and be turned into another man" (1 Sam. 10:6–7). The account ends: "Therefore it became a proverb, 'Is Saul also among the prophets?'" Saul sends messengers to take David, but "When they saw the company of prophets prophesying, and Samuel standing as head over them, the Spirit of God came over the messengers ... and they also prophesied." Saul's next two groups are similarly affected. Finally, Saul goes himself, "and he too stripped off his clothes, and he too prophesied before Samuel, and lay naked all that day and all that night. Hence it is said: 'Is Saul also among the prophets?'" (1 Sam. 19:24).

Ecstatic prophecy, unlike classical (literary) prophecy, is widely attested cross-culturally. For example, the Egyptian "Travels of Wen-Amon" notes that "while he was making offering to his gods, the god seized one of his youths and made him possessed." Num. 24:16 introduces Balaam by saying that the spirit of God possessed him and by describing his position: "falling down but having his eyes uncovered."

This type of prophecy can be and was artificially induced. From a shrine in Anatolia dating to the 5th millennium B.C.E., archaeologists have recovered an opium pipe. In Ugarit, wine was used; in South America, psylocibin, toad skins, and so on; and at Delphi, noxious fumes.

Next we see the shift from ecstatic to pre-classical prophesy. The "sons of the prophets" who travel in bands (1 Sam. 10:5) and prophesy with one voice (1 Kings 22:12) may have served as the transition group. These prophetic bands may be directed by a teacher (cf. 1 Sam. 19–20, in which the leader is Samuel). Elijah's band apparently preserved the traditions of their teacher. The prophetic guilds may have worn external signs of office, such as shaved heads; cf. 2 Kings 2:23–25: "Some small boys came out of the city and jeered at [Elisha], saying: 'go up, you baldhead. Go up, you baldhead.' And he turned around, and when he saw them he cursed them in the name of the Lord. And two she-bears came out of the wood and tore up forty-two of the boys." Separation from the group: When an individual prophesies apart from the group, pre-classical prophesy formally begins. This is the case with Micaiah, the son of Imlah, of whom Ahab, the king of Israel, states: "I hate him, for he never prophecies good concerning me, but evil," (1 Kings 22).

Elijah, the major pre-classical prophet, is cast as a new Moses. Like Moses and Joshua, he parts water (the Jordan, in 2 Kings 2:7). Like Moses, he experiences a theophany at Horeb (1 Kings 19:8ff.). Elijah builds an altar with twelve stones (1Kings 18:30); Moses constructs an altar flanked by twelve pillars (Exod. 24:4). Elijah performs a sacrifice, the altar is consumed by fire, and the people bow (1 Kings 18:38ff.); Moses offers a sacrifice after consecrating his altar, the fire consumes the offering, and the people bow (Lev. 9:24). Like Moses, Elijah has no tomb. He is carried to heaven in a fiery chariot (hence the spiritual; see 2 Kings 2:11). In later legend, Elijah associated with Enoch, who also never "dies." The prophet Malachi, the last of the canon's classical prophets, predicts his return "before the great and terrible 'day of the Lord' comes" (Mal. 4:5 [3:23]).

Elijah's task is to prevent the people from succumbing to Baalism, sponsored by King Ahab of Israel and, especially, by his Sidonian wife, Jezebel. The predominant Canaanite deity is Baal, often accompanied by his consort(s) Anath, Ashtoreth/Ishtar/Astarte. Against their worship not only Elijah but also the classical prophets Amos and Hosea struggle, as we shall see in the next lecture. ■

Suggested Reading

Commentaries in series listed in the bibliography.

Michael D. Coogan (ed.), *The Oxford History of the Biblical World*.

Questions to Consider

1. What is the most effective way of overcoming temptations to syncretism: incorporation of competing language (the psalms), prophetic polemic, political persecution, or other?

2. In what way is madness culturally constructed? Is according a prophetic role to one who "raves" a helpful means of giving people who behave in nontraditional ways a place in society?

The Prophets and the Fall of the North
(1 Kgs. 16–2 Kgs. 17, Amos, Hosea)
Lecture 18

> The theophany that Elijah experiences is an anti-Baal polemic because Baal is a nature god manifested through rain, manifested through storms and in thunder. ... Following all these natural signs comes a stillness, and it's in that stillness that God speaks to Elijah. There is the difference between the God of Israel and Baal.

Elijah contrasts the powers of YHWH and Baal. The Canaanite nature god cannot provide food, but in the midst of famine, YHWH's prophet is miraculously fed, and he can miraculously feed others, as he does for the widow of Zarephath. On Mt. Horeb, Elijah witnesses wind, earthquake, then fire, but YHWH comes in the silence: He is neither in, nor controlled by, nature (1 Kings 19:1–18). Yearly, Mot (death) overcomes Baal, but Anath revives him with appropriate rituals. Elijah raises a dead boy, while the "dying/rising god" cannot resurrect himself.

In addition to calling rulers to account, pre-classical prophets also sanction political events. Elijah's successor, Elisha, arranges the coup that deposes Ahab and places Jehu on the throne. The prophetess Huldah legitimates the Book of Deuteronomy. Prophetic signs can solidify political symbols. By the separation of Solomon's kingdom, with Solomon's son Rehoboam continuing the Davidic line in Judea in the South and Jereboam I ruling in Israel, the North (1 Kings 11:26ff.) receives prophetic warrant. The prophet Ahijah states that Solomon had to be punished: "Because he has forsaken me, and worshiped Ashtoreth the goddess of the Sidonians, Chemosh the god of Moab ... and has not walked in my ways, doing what is right in my sight ... as David his father did" (1 Kgs.12:33). The prophet sanctions the split by symbolizing it: "Ahijah laid hold of the new garment that was on him, and tore it into twelve pieces."

The twelve "minor prophets" are collected together after the major latter prophets (Isaiah, Jeremiah, and Ezekiel). This collection is also called "The Book of the Twelve." The minor prophets are: Hosea, Joel, Amos, Obadiah, Jonah, Micah, Nahum, Habakkuk, Zephaniah, Haggai, Zechariah, and Malachi. The order is roughly chronological, from earliest to latest. The Book of the Twelve equals the length of each major prophetic scroll.

Prophetic rhetoric, arresting expressions and evocations of Israel's history, these devices continue the covenant practice of self-criticism. Amos opens with a series of pronouncements against Israel's neighbors: Judah, Edom, Moab, Ammon, and so on. The nations listed first are condemned for their treatment of outsiders (usually Israel and Judah). Israel and Judah are then condemned for internal social oppression. Israel's crime is more heinous in that the people reject God's blessings. Amos 2:10–11 invokes the liberation from Egypt and the early days of Canaan. Amos adopts the rhetorical forms of cultic proclamation but announces the opposite of what was expected: "Woe to you who desire the day of the Lord! Why would you have the day of the Lord? It is darkness and not light." (5:18ff.).

Amos, one of the earliest prophets.

Devices associated with the wisdom tradition (Proverbs, Ecclesiastes, Job): (1) Rhetorical questions and images from nature: "Do two walk together unless they have made an appointment? Does a lion roar in the forest when he has no prey?" (Amos 3:3–4). (2) Comparisons: "Thus says the Lord: 'As the shepherd rescues from the mouth of the lion two legs, or a piece of an ear, so shall the people of Israel who dwell in Samaria be rescued, with the corner of a couch and part of a bed'" (Amos 3:11–12). (3) Striking characterizations excoriated the upper class: "Hear this word, you cows of Bashan ... who oppress the poor, who crush the needy, who say to their husbands: 'Bring that we may drink ... '" (Amos 4:1ff.). Of particular concern to the prophets was religious complacency, people who observe the rituals while ignoring the poor in their midst.

Amos, although from Judah, proclaimed his message in the cultic shrines of Israel during the reign of Jereboam II (787–747), a time of economic prosperity. He identifies himself (1:1) as "among the shepherds of Tekoa." With only two exceptions, the *Tanakh* uses *ro'eh* for shepherd; Amos uses *noqed*. Comparative philology and Ugaritic cognates indicate that the *noqed* is a shepherd who cares for temple flocks destined for sacrifice. Amos divorces himself from such connections: "I am no prophet, nor one of the sons of the prophets ... [i.e., a member of a prophetic guild], but I am a herder and a dresser of sycamore trees" (7:14). The line may suggest that Amos is a seasonal or migrant worker.

Hosea's initial activity coincides with the last year of Jereboam II (747 B.C.E.) and the Syro-Ephraimite war (Hos. 5:8–14, cf. 2 Kings 15:27–30). In 734–732, Syria and Ephraim/Israel united against Assyria, but Assyria prevailed, and Israel was subjugated by the Assyrian king Tiglath-Pilesar III. Hos. 12:12f. describes "Jacob" as "Fleeing to the land of Aram; there Israel did service for a wife, and for a wife he herded sheep." Jacob's desire is transformed into an unproductive Syrian alliance. Hosea adapts traditions of Israel's past. Hos. 2:1ff. offers an allegory of Israel's covenantal history. Reformation appears to be beyond both the ability and the will of priesthood, court, and people; only destruction will make renewal possible. The allegory evokes the Baal cult: "In that day, says the Lord, you will call me 'my husband' and no longer will you call me 'my Baal'" (2:16–17).

Let's look at the fall of the North. Hos. 5:14 accurately observes, "I will carry off and none shall return." In 725–724, Israel violated its treaty with Assyria and turned to Egypt for protection. Sargon II of Assyria then began a siege that culminated in 722 when Samaria fell and Sargon deported about five percent of the population (see 2 Kings 17). The Assyrian conquest is confirmed by external documentation. An inscription from Sargon II concerning the conquering of Samaria includes the statement: "I led away as booty 27,290 inhabitants of it." Sargon II's inscription goes on: "with the tribes of Tamud, Ibadidi, Marsimanu, and Halapa, the Arabs who live far away, in the desert ... I deported their survivors and settled them in Samaria." They "feared the Lord, but also served their own gods, after the manner of the nations from among whom they had been carried away ... So they do to this day" (2 Kgs. 17:29–41). ■

Suggested Reading

Major commentaries in the series listed in the bibliography.

Questions to Consider

1. Have either political or religious rhetoric changed much over the past two-and-a-half millennia?

2. What elements need to be in place for a culture to survive geographical displacement?

3. In the shared system of governance among kings, priests, and prophets, how is balance maintained?

The Southern Kingdom
(Isaiah, Deuteronomy, 2 Kings 18–23)
Lecture 19

> The combination of the people moved in by the Assyrians and the indigenous population remaining in the land comprise a new group of people who become known as Samaritans.

The Northern Kingdom fell, but both its memory and its reconfiguration continued to affect the identity of Judah. The resettled peoples in the North intermarried with remaining Israelites. They came to be called "Samaritans" from Israel's capital, Samaria, and they will become the enemies of the people in the South. The "10 tribes" are lost to history but preserved in legends. The people of the South yearn for the reconstitution of all the tribes, and from this, certain legends develop: They are the Native Americans; they are the British (from *Berit* [covenant] and *ish* [man]—a false etymology); they were relocated to China, India, or Afghanistan; or they were reintegrated into the covenant community in the Messianic age.

Israel, compared to Judah, has a less visible theological system. With the emphasis on only the Mosaic covenant, Israel perhaps believed that with expulsion, the suzerain was no longer protecting the vassal. The people may have lacked a strong clergy. They lacked a viable "canon." Distinctions between the exile of the Israelites and the exile of the Judeans by Nebuchadnezzar. Assyria fractured ethnic groups in exile; the Babylonians established exiled groups in self-governing neighborhoods. Assyria was not conquered until the Babylonian campaigns of 612, over a century after Samaria fell; Babylonian captivity lasted forty-eight years.

Scholars argue that the biblical book entitled "Isaiah" is a composite representing at least three prophetic voices addressing different historical settings. First Isaiah, chapters 1–24, 28–39. The "first Isaiah" flourished during the second half of the 8th century. The first Isaiah had at least two children, each with a symbolic name (cf. Hosea's children): She'ar-Jashub

(7:3), "a remnant will return," and Maher-Shalal-Hash-Baz (8:1–4), "The Spoil speeds, the prey hastens." His "call" (Isa. 6) occurs "in the year King Uzziah died" (742), after a reign of forty years. His prophetic "school" (cf. 8:16–17) continued into the post-exilic period.

Along with the various rhetorical forms and images associated with Amos and Hosea (woe oracles, the adulterous wife, personification of the rich as indolent women), Isaiah develops the parable (cf. 2 Sam. 12:1–12). Most famous of these is the "parable of the vineyard" (5:1–7), in which God is the planter and Judah the vineyard that fails. For Isaiah, the golden age is not the wilderness period (as it was for Hosea), but Davidic Jerusalem, and it is Jerusalem he seeks to save. Isaiah, seeking Judean political neutrality, counsels against involvement in the Syro-Ephraimite War (7:1–16; see 2 Kings 20) through the oracle of Immanuel: "Behold a young woman has conceived and shall bear a son, and shall call his name Immanuel. This child shall eat curds and honey when he knows how to refuse the evil and choose the good."

Isaiah, the first major prophet from the Southern Kingdom.

References to a "virgin" birth derive from the Septuagint, which renders the Hebrew "young woman" as *parthenos*. Isaiah 9 and 11 describe an ideal king; the imagery develops into messianic desiderata. Judean royal theology also contributes to messianic speculation.

Like Amos and, especially, Hosea, it is not clear whether Isaiah expects the people to repent. "Go and say to this people: 'Hear and hear, but do not understand; see and see, but do not perceive … ' until the cities lie waste, without inhabitants" (6:9–13). Rather than prophesying total destruction, Isaiah promulgates a "remnant theology," as his son's name, She'ar-Jashub (and see 10:20–23), suggests.

King Hezekiah (c. 704), likely prompted by Isaiah, instituted a series of religious and political reforms (2 Kings 18). Among these reforms was the symbolic end to vassalage by stopping sacrifices to the Assyrian emperor. Domestically, cultic reforms included the razing of "high places" and "sacred poles" and the removal from the Temple of Nehushtan the bronze serpent that Moses had made for apotropaic cures (18:4). Public policy reforms included the Jerusalem water conduit (Hezekiah's tunnel, the Siloam tunnel, a 1,700-foot excavation through solid rock).

The reforms ended with King Hezekiah's death. His successor, Manasseh, returned Judah to vassal status (2 Kings 21). Manasseh also reintroduced apostasy: rebuilding the high places and erecting sacred poles, constructing altars to Baal, and so on.

Josiah, Manasseh's grandson, attempted a second reform based on the laws of Deuteronomy (2 Kings 22–23). Deuteronomy is ostensibly Moses's last will and testament, only discovered during Josiah's Temple renovations (22:8–10). The prophetess Huldah, when visited by a consortium of priests, (indirectly) proclaims the book to be authentic (22:14–20). Deuteronomy abolishes previously legitimate altars (Deut. 12:1–31; 12:5–6). It disenfranchises the Levites, who had presided over the local shrines. It centralizes the cult in Jerusalem (the Samaritan Pentateuch locates the centralization in Samaria, on Mt. Gerizim). Of particular concern are monarchical interests: the divine legitimation of the king. He is exhorted (17:18) to "write for himself in a book a copy of this law." The LXX translates "copy" as *Deuteronomion*, "Second law."

Deuteronomy's notable contributions to biblical law include: (1) Promoting the education of children by inculcation, cf. 6:7: "You shall teach them [the Laws] diligently to your children, and you shall talk of them when you sit in your house, and when you walk by the way, and when you lie down, and when you rise up. And you shall bind them for a sign upon your hand, and they shall be for frontlets between your eyes; and you shall write them upon the doorposts of your house, and upon your gates." (2) The sign and frontlets are *Tefillin* or phylacteries, two small square leather boxes containing scriptural passages worn on the forehead and left arm. And (3) The doorpost/gate reference is to the *Mezuzah* (Hebrew for "doorpost"), a case containing Deut. 6:4–9 (the "Shema"); 11:13–21, and El Shaddai.

The hopes created by the Deuteronomic reform were dashed when Josiah, having reneged on his participation in the Syrian-Egyptian alliance, is then killed by Pharaoh Neco at Megiddo. The failure of the reform and the rise of Babylon set the stage for the prophecies of Jeremiah and for the Babylonian exile, the topics of the next lecture. ■

Suggested Reading

Commentaries in series listed in the bibliography.

Michael D. Coogan, (ed.), *The Oxford History of the Biblical World*.

Questions to Consider

1. What are the benefits, and the dangers, of interpreting prophetic oracles outside their original historical situations?

2. How does the international scene affect Judean policies, both political and religious?

3. How and to what extent does Deuteronomy respond to the prophetic calls for social justice?

Babylonian Exile
(2 Kgs. 24–25, Jeremiah, Isaiah 40–55, Ezekiel)
Lecture 20

I often think that we should take pity on those poor prophets who had to speak to the covenant community in the southern kingdom of Judah. Their kings and their people were convinced that there was no way the country would ever fall. They had the promises to David.

The siege of Judah: "In the 14th year of King Hezekiah, Sennacherib King of Assyria came up against the fortified cities of Judah and took them" (2 Kings 18:13). Recognizing the disaster of the Kingdom of Israel, the South had to respond. To prevent catastrophe, King Hezekiah pays enormous tribute, including stripping the gold from the Temple, but the siege prevails. Herodotus (*Hist.* II.131) attests that the Assyrians suffered a defeat on the borders of Egypt because their equipment was ruined by some ravenous field mice, a notice some scholars connect with the Judean situation. Sennacherib's own version implies that after a successful attack on Jerusalem, Hezekiah agreed to increased tribute, which he would send directly to Nineveh. The Deuteronomic historian attributes the lifting of the siege to divine intervention: "And that night the angel of the Lord went forth and slew 185,000 men in the camp of the Assyrians" (2 Kings 19:34; cf. Isa. 36–39). Judean theologians concluded that the royal grant protected Jerusalem (Isa. 10:24ff.).

Babylon defeats the Egyptian-Assyrian coalition at the Battle of Carchemish in 605 (see Jer. 46:2; 2 Kings 24). Judah is now under Babylonian control. Jehoiakim, King of Judah, rebels after a three-year submission but dies (in 598) before Babylon retaliates. Jehoiakim's son, Jehoiachin (Jeconiah), surrenders to Nebuchadnezzar (Nebuchadrezzar) in 597 (see Jer. 21:2; 2 Kings 24; this surrender is attested in Babylonian records). Probably between 3,000 and 10,000 people are then deported.

We see the end of the Judean monarchy when Mattaniah (probably another son of Josiah) is made king and renamed Zedekiah to symbolize his vassal status (1 Chr. 3). Zedekiah seeks an alliance with Egypt (Jer. 17; 1 Kings 25; Ezek. 17). In retaliation, Nebuchadnezzar destroys Jerusalem, forces a second deportation, takes the Temple valuables to Babylon, and executes Zedekiah. Gedaliah, a friend to Jeremiah (Jer. 39–40), is appointed governor but assassinated by a member of the royal family.

Given this dismal situation, Jeremiah reflects an intense spiritual struggle. His oracles are juxtaposed with events in his life such that his personal tragedies mirror the nation's doom. His "temple sermon" provokes a judicial hearing. His prophesying put his life in danger: Manasseh probably executed prophets (2 Kgs. 21:1b), and King Jehoiakim certainly did (2 Kgs. 26:20–33; Jer. 2:20). His solution to Judah's failings is a "new covenant" (31:31ff.), in which YHWH "Will put my law within them, and I will write it upon their hearts ..."

After Gedaliah's murder, Jeremiah and his scribe, Baruch, are taken by Judean refugees to Egypt. The Book of Lamentations, although traditionally attributed to him, manifests his sorrow but not his themes or style. From Jeremiah's exile develops the legend that the ark, last seen when Solomon placed it in the Holy of Holies (1 Kings 8), was brought to Egypt. Second Maccabees 2:4ff. suggests that Jeremiah hid the ark on Mt. Nebo and proclaimed, "The place shall be unknown until God gathers his people together again and shows his mercy."

Ezekiel proclaimed both invective and hope to the Babylonian exiles c. 593–563. Probably part of the first deportation of 597, Ezekiel found an exilic community confident that rescue was imminent and the Temple, inviolable. These Judeans linked their position with that of Abraham: "The word of the Lord came to me, 'Son of man, the inhabitants of the waste places ... keep saying, 'Abraham was only one man, yet he got possession of the land; but we are many; the land is surely given to us to possess'" (33:24). Ezekiel insists that this view is incorrect; the people are not yet deserving of redemption. His message is less one of consolation than of justification. The people's apostasy caused YHWH to bring about the exile. Redemption will follow repentance (36:24): "I will take you from the nations, and gather you from all the countries, and bring you into your own land." But this will occur only "after many days ... in the later years" (38:8–16).

Earlier prophets and the Deuteronomic history spoke of sin as a corporate problem, and its results could be inherited (e.g., the sins of Manasseh precipitate the exile). Ezekiel stresses individual responsibility: "The son shall not suffer for the iniquity of the father, nor shall the father suffer for the iniquity of the son; the righteousness of the righteous shall be upon himself, and the wickedness of the wicked shall be on himself" (18:20).

Ezekiel's prophecy is enhanced by highly symbolic terminology (wheels within wheels [the "chariot vision"]; the valley of the dry bones). He also engages in symbolic actions (Ezekiel is commanded not to mourn the death of his wife, to remain in particular positions for extremely long periods of time). Perhaps the intensity, if not complete oddity, of his pronouncements and visions is best seen in the context of exilic trauma. His visions foreshadow changes in prophetic language as prophets find increasing resistance to their proclamations: after exile, what more could be threatened?

The Second Isaiah offers a message of consolation. YHWH, not Marduk, controls history. Because exile was predicted, prophecy of restoration is also credible: "A voice cries, 'In the wilderness prepare the way of the Lord; make straight in the desert a highway for our God'" (40:3). The return of the exiles will be a new Exodus (Isa. 43). Babylonian gods will go into captivity as Babylon is destroyed (Isa. 46–48).

YHWH's universal sovereignty and suffering servant. Isa. 44:5 anticipates universal recognition of God and the covenant community: "This one will say, 'I am the Lord's'; another will call himself by the name of Jacob." The "suffering servant" motif extends the *diaspora* promise: "I will give you as a light to the nations, that my salvation will reach to the end of the earth ..." (49:1–6; cf. 42:1–4; 51:4ff.). Isaiah's image of Abraham reverses that in Ezekiel. Isa. 51:2–3 reads: "Look to Abraham your father and to Sarah who bore you; for when he was but one I called him, and I blessed him and made him many."

YHWH appoints Cyrus of Persia ("God's anointed," Heb: *Messiah*) to defeat Babylon (Isa. 44:24–45:13). In 539 B.C.E., the Babylonian king Nabonidus flees, and the Persian army takes Babylon peacefully. Cyrus will, in 538, sponsor an edict to permit those in exile to return home. This practice is confirmed by the Cyrus Cylinder, dated to 528 B.C.E. ∎

Suggested Reading

Commentaries in series listed in the bibliography.

Michael D. Coogan, (ed.), *The Oxford History of the Biblical World*.

Questions to Consider

1. Are references to other nations in a universal monotheism indicative of inclusion, co-optation, colonialism, or all three?

2. How does one distinguish between a theology of hope and a theology of self-deception?

3. How does "religion" (defined as you will) in a *diaspora* or in exile differ from religion in the homeland?

Restoration and Theocracy
(Isaiah 56–55, Ezra–Nehemiah, Haggai, Zechariah, Malachi, Ruth, Jonah)
Lecture 21

> When King Cyrus of Persia promulgated his edict in 538 B.C.E., permitting the Jews in exile in Babylon to return home, great excitement no doubt occurred. ... with enormous hope people left and returned home. Unfortunately, things were not as they had hoped they would be. The destruction that Nebuchadnezzar had brought when he destroyed Jerusalem had not been repaired. The city was in ruins. Moreover, the people who had not been taken into exile resented the return of those from Babylon.

The Cyrus Cylinder (cf. Isa. 44:28; 45:1; 47ff; Ezra 1:2–4; 2 Chron. 36:23: Ezra 6:3–5) states: "I returned to [these] sacred cities on the other side of the Tigris, the sanctuaries of which have been ruins for a long time, the images which [used] to live therein, and established for them permanent sanctuaries. I gathered all their inhabitants and returned their habitations." Under Persian rule, the Judeans are encouraged to rebuild their Temple with funds provided from the royal treasury. Cyrus allows the return of Temple vessels plundered by Babylon (2 Kings 24:13). Persia's tactics were politically expedient: toleration of a subject nation's cultural practices and limited autonomous governance. Both fostered stability and provided a bulwark against the growing Greek threat. The Jewish military colony at Elephantine notes that Cambyses (529–522) did not damage their temple despite destroying "all the temples of the gods of the Egyptians."

Darius I (522–486) divides the empire into twenty satrapies; Judah belongs to Avar Nahal, "beyond the river." Persia offered satrapies substantial autonomy, developed an efficient means of communication, and facilitated the flourishing of commerce. The satraps (first the Davidide Zerubbabel, then the courtier Nehemiah) were chosen with regard to local concerns.

For many, the Jerusalem anticipated by the Second Isaiah was a severe disappointment. "Zion has become a wilderness, Jerusalem a desolation; O holy and beautiful house where our fathers praised you have been burned by fire, and all our pleasant places have become ruins" (Isa. 64:10–12). Second Isaiah's universalism ("light to the nations") transforms into siege mentality: "I have trodden the wine press alone ... I trod them with my anger and trampled them in my wrath" (Isa. 63:3). Haggai deplores the languishing of the cult and the poor condition of the Temple: "Who is left among you who saw this house in its former glory? How do you see it now? Is it not in your sight as nothing?" (2:3). The Temple's rebuilding did not, contrary to expectations, usher in an age of prosperity. Hag. 1:6ff. and Zech. 6:8–9 reveal a people who are starving, freezing, and poor. Many questioned the value of serving YHWH. As Malachi opens, "'I have loved you,' says the Lord; but you say, 'How have you loved us?'"

Contributing to the disappointment was the failed restoration government. Haggai exhorts the priest (Joshua) and the governor (Zerubbabel) to take courage and work. Ezra and Zechariah attest to their collaboration. Zerubbabel disappears from history and leaves no heir. Persian authorities may have removed or even executed him; the Davidic line is lost here. Levites sought to regain power wrested from them under Deuteronomic reform. Aaronides still worked to consolidate the power accorded them by the P source/the Babylonian Judean establishment.

The struggle for power was ultimately won by the Aaronide priests. The legitimacy of the priesthood was established in the symbolic rites of investiture (comparable to a royal coronation) involving Joshua (Zech. 3:1–9). Priestly rule is epitomized in the authority accorded Ezra by his own community and by the Persian government. For Malachi, the task of religious and moral instruction passes from the prophets, whose authority rested on revelation, to those entrusted with a hereditary commission, the priests.

By the Persian period, classical prophecy was on the verge of collapse (Ps. 74:9; Lam. 2:9; Zech. 13:2–5): "I will remove from the land the prophets. ... And if anyone again appears as a prophet, his father and mother who bore him will say to him, 'You shall not live, for you speak lies in the name of the Lord … '" The movement's demise followed the exile: What more could prophets threaten, after exile, the destruction of the Temple, Persian rule, and famine? Prophetic promises, such as those of the Second Isaiah, failed. Sin prospered, and righteousness was ineffectual (Mal. 3:14; Eccl. 9:13–15). Malachi was unable to take for granted even the most basic element of Israelite theology: God's love for the community.

A contributing factor was the demise of the monarchy. Government was in the hands of priests and their Persian sponsors. Whom was the prophet to condemn? The priests were themselves associated with divine sanction, and the Persians did not care. The post-exilic period needed unity, which prophetic argument threatened to undermine; without the countering force of the throne, prophetic critique would create political imbalance.

Genealogy and ethnic identity become increasingly important as Judea recognizes itself to be part of an empire. Ezra legislates that Judean men divorce their foreign

Jonah preaching to the Ninevites.

Boaz and Ruth.

wives; genealogy becomes increasingly important (cf. 1, 2 Chron.). Likely written to combat this ethnocentrism are the novellas of Ruth and Jonah. The novellas offer positive views of gentiles but implicitly warn against assimilation. Ruth, continually identified as "Ruth the Moabite," seduces Boaz on the threshing floor, a scene reminiscent of Genesis 19. Ruth the Moabite becomes David's great-grandmother. Jonah—attempting to escape the divine command to preach to Nineveh—is first tossed overboard, then swallowed by a great fish, and ultimately left to the burning sun while the Assyrians repent. ■

Suggested Reading

Commentaries in series listed in the bibliography.

Michael D. Coogan, (ed.), *The Oxford History of the Biblical World.*

Kenneth M. Craig, *The Poetics of Jonah: Art in the Service of Ideology*, 2nd ed.

Questions to Consider

1. How are moral values promulgated in circumstances of despair?

2. What adaptations do cultures make when they become part of an external empire?

3. What prompted the post-exilic stress on genealogy and the concern for assimilation?

4. How might Ruth be compared to Abraham? What are the implications of her Moabite ancestry?

5. Is Jonah a comedy or a tragedy?

Wisdom Literature
(Song of Songs, Proverbs, Ecclesiastes, Job)
Lecture 22

When we look at the wisdom tradition, we find an amazing influence by and indeed respect for the international community, the international wisdom community. We've already seen this earlier in discussions of Solomon's court, where people from the nations would come to experience the wisdom that he himself promulgated and the wisdom of the other people he brought into his court.

The international implications of empire, while manifested in the xenophobia of Ezra and Nehemiah and the irresistible universalism of YHWH according to Ruth and Jonah, take on a third form: "wisdom," a tradition well established in the Near East. Biblical wisdom is partially epitomized by the books ascribed to Solomon: Song of Songs (Song of Solomon, Canticles), Proverbs, and Ecclesiastes.

Song of Songs (Song of Solomon, Canticles) is actually less a text of "wisdom" teaching than a celebration of the joys of love, emotional as well as physical. Its literary parallels are less Proverbs and Ecclesiastes than Egyptian love poetry. The song's overt sensuality complements the earthiness of Genesis and Judges, as does its powerful woman's voice. Under Hellenistic influence, the song became regarded as a spiritual allegory of the love between Israel and God or the Church and the Christ. Some interpreters propose that parts may be parody (e.g., "Your hair is like a flock of goats streaming down Mt. Gilead" [4:1]). Current multicultural readings call attention to the fact that the Hebrew can bear either of two translations of "I am black and/but beautiful."

Proverbs, a cross-cultural form for promoting proper attitudes and behaviors, receives divine sanction by Lady Wisdom herself (1–9). The proverbs encourage (male) readers to cleave to Lady Wisdom and avoid the paths of Strange (foreign, adulterous) Woman (Dame Folly). Wisdom as a character is increasingly developed in the Old Testament Apocrypha/Deuterocanonical writings (e.g., Wisdom of Solomon). She finds herself contributing to the *Shekinah*, the feminine manifestation of the divine, in Judaism, and the *Logos*, the pre-existent form of the incarnate Christ, depicted in the Prologue of the Gospel of John.

Ecclesiastes (Qoheleth, "leader of the assembly") negotiates life in a world of ennui. Tradition suggests that the Song of Songs is the product of Solomon's youth; Proverbs, of his adult prime; and Ecclesiastes, of his age. The text combines a pessimistic view of life ("Vanity of vanities ... all is vanity" [12:8]; "there is nothing new under the sun" [1:9]) with utilitarian advice following from it (eat, drink, and be merry [cf. 9:7]; rejoice in your youth [cf. 11:9]). Everything has its season (3:1–8); risk taking is advisable ("Cast your bread upon the waters" [11:1]); fear God (12:13, perhaps from the hand of a later editor).

Robert Gordis states, "There is not, nor can there be, universal agreement on such major issues as the structure, the unity, and the basic meaning of the book, or even on such relatively minor questions as its style, date, and origin." Perhaps the book offers less a solution to the problem of suffering than an opportunity for readers to engage the question. Various appropriations include Goethe's *Faust*; MacLeish's *J.B.*; H. G. Wells's *The Undying Fire*; and Heinlein's *Job, A Comedy*.

The traditional interpretation, premised on the prose frame, views Job as an ideal figure who continually engages in pious action; accepts the loss of his property and the death of his children with faithful resignation; refuses to follow his wife's advice, "Curse God and die"; repents of any possible doubt; and submits before divine majesty. A variant view makes Job an existentialist "everyman" demanding meaning from a chaotic world. Appropriately, this Job is not Jewish or Israelite (he descends from Esau). This is the Job of G. K. Chesterton: "The *Iliad* is great because all life is a battle; the *Odyssey* is great because all life is a journey; the Book of Job is great because all life is a riddle." Some see the book as a satire depicting a hypocritical protagonist who confirms the Satan's accusations (pious when rewarded; argumentative when his life is destroyed; pious again when the opportunity of restoration is presented) and a tyrannical, unstable God who demands worship as a form of extortion. Perhaps Job is a realist who is sure only of his righteousness but recognizes that the world lacks justice. This is the Job who tells God: "I know you can do all things ..." but, so knowing, pities humanity: "I mourn in dust and ashes" (42:2–3). There may be mutually exclusive Jobs: one from the prologue and one from the poem, with the epilogue fitting both.

The prosaic Job remains faithful, "Then Job arose, and rent his robe, and shaved his head, and fell on the ground, and worshiped. And he said, 'Naked came I from my mother's womb, and naked I shall return. The Lord gave, and the Lord has taken away; blessed be the name of the Lord.' In all this, Job did not sin, or charge God with wrong" (1:20). The poetic Job bewails his fate, curses the Deity (e.g., 16:11), curses his birth, and longs for his death (from the opening line).

Job and his friends.

How are we to understand God, who permits Job's suffering, then condemns Job's friends for defending traditional theology in insisting on a correlation between faith and fate? Eliphaz appeals to mystical visions (4, 15) and describes suffering as a form of discipline and a mark of divine love (5). Eliphaz also echoes the Deuteronomic view that "the sins of the fathers are visited upon the sons" (22) and bolsters it with appeal to the corporate community's mutual responsibility. Bildad, invoking traditional wisdom (8), and Zophar, appealing to esoteric wisdom (11), recapitulate Eliphaz's arguments. Elihu adds that suffering serves to deter sin (33, 36), such as pride. Does God favor Job because he speaks from experience rather than theory? Or is the Deity simply arbitrary?

Even further complicating interpretation are the whirlwind speeches (38:1–40:5; 40:6–41:34). Does the whirlwind indicate that God is unknowable, yet operating purposefully? "Where were you when I laid the foundations of the earth, tell me, if you have understanding. Who determined its measurements, surely you know" (38:4). Might the point be less what is said but the theophany itself, that the divine is not indifferent (42:5: "I have heard of you by the hearing of the ear, but now my eye sees you")? Or is it all just sound and fury?

Job 13:15 yields three mutually exclusive translations: KJV: "Though he slay me, yet I will trust him"; RSV: "Behold he will slay me, I have no hope"; and Anchor Bible: "He may slay me, I'll not quaver." Job 19:25 traditionally reads, "For I know that my redeemer lives ..." but the translation is uncertain. ■

Suggested Reading

Marcia Falk, *Love Lyrics from the Bible, The Song of Songs: A New Translation and Interpretation*.

Roland E. Murphy, *The Tree of Life: An Exploration of Biblical Wisdom Literature*.

Questions to Consider

1. Why would ancient Israel canonize pessimistic wisdom, such as Ecclesiastes and Job?

2. Is the God of Job the God of the *Akedah*? Of Jephthah? Of Saul?

3. How does the scribe, responsible for wisdom, relate to king, priest, and prophet?

Life in the Diaspora
(Genesis 30, 37–50; Esther; Daniel 1–6)
Lecture 23

> The Babylonian exile gave rise to the *diaspora*, the "dispersion" of the Judeans now known as "Jews" to places outside their homeland.

The least controversial figure in Job is *ha-satan*, "the accuser." In Zechariah, as in Job, *the* Satan ("the accuser") is the heavenly prosecuting agent whose task is to weed out evil and hypocrisy. Isa. 14:12–15 contributes to the mythic development: "How you are fallen from heaven, O day star, son of Dawn ... You who said in your heart, 'I will ascend to heaven above the stars of God ... I will make myself like the most high ...' But you are brought down to Sheol, to the depths of the pit." Ugaritic texts speak of Shahar, god of Dawn, and his son Helal, Morning Star. Isaiah identifies the Babylonian king with Canaanite gods. "Day star" or "light bringer" is, in Latin, Lucifer. The "tales of the diaspora" present as heroes figures representing the wisdom tradition: Daniel and Mordecai. It is to the Books of Daniel and Esther, and to a discussion of Jewish life outside Israel, we next turn.

The Book of Esther may well have taken shape during the Persian period. However, even if King Ahasueros is to be associated with Xerxes I, there is no external record of his having a Jewish queen or prime minister. Esther exists in Hebrew as well as two Greek versions. The LXX version (the Deuterocanonical text [Old Testament Apocrypha]) has six major additions that give the story an overt religious component: the mention of God over fifty times, an explicit distaste for intermarriage (cf. Ezra and Nehemiah), concern for dietary regulations, and so on. Compounding the difficulties of determining an "original" story is the absence of Esther from Qumran.

In a variant of the convention, the Book of Esther offers rival wives (Sarah and Hagar, Rachel and Leah, Hannah and Peninnah), but the rivalry is presented through behavioral differences rather than through personal conflict: Esther only appears, can only appear, after Vashti is dismissed. Vashti refuses the king's order to appear at his banquet. Vashti refuses to leave her own banquet to attend the king (her rationale—disgust at being an object of display for drunken men, involvement with her own party, mean-spiritedness—is never explained). Vashti's refusal prompts a law that "all women will give honor to their husbands, high and low alike" (1:20). Vashti's refusal results in a law mandating her banishment, i.e., Ahasueros writes into law the confirmation of her refusal.

Ahasueros is less malevolent than inept: He holds a banquet for "all his officials and ministers, the army of Persia and Media and the nobles and governors of the provinces," the entire infrastructure of the empire, for six months. He is almost always drinking or drunk. He chooses a bride not for political alliance but on the basis of a "beauty" contest in which each candidate spends a year marinating in myrrh, followed by one night with the king. From this contest, he decides to marry Esther, even though he knows nothing of her background. "Esther did not reveal her people or kindred, for Mordecai had charged her not to tell" (2:10). Yet Mordecai insists such silence will not, ultimately, help (Est. 4:13). The danger to the Jews comes first from Haman, the prime minister, whose hatred of Mordecai, Esther's uncle or cousin, extends to all Jews, then from those people in the empire who are willing to carry out the genocidal decree. The enmity between Haman and Mordecai may even have been predicted: Mordecai is a Benjaminite, as was Saul (Est. 2:5; 1 Sam. 9:1; each is explicitly identified as the "son of Kish"). Haman is an Agagite (Est. 9:24), and Saul's sparing of Agag and his taking of booty contribute to his tragedy (1 Sam. 15). Esther does save her people. She, unlike Vashti, comes unbidden to the king. Further, she invites her husband to a banquet in which she manages to place Haman in a compromising position. He is then hanged on the gallows he erected for Mordecai. The book consequently suggests that diaspora communities need to be aware that they may suddenly find themselves no longer welcome in the land they have made their home (one recollects the Exodus), and that even if the authorities wish to protect them, the local population may not.

By king's command and Esther's instruction, "The Jews struck down all their enemies with the sword, slaughtering and destroying them, and did as they

Esther accuses Haman.

pleased to those who hated them. In the citadel city of Susa the Jews killed and destroyed five-hundred people" (9:5–6). "The other Jews who were in the king's provinces also gathered to defend their lives, and gained relief from their enemies, and killed seventy-five thousand of those who hated them; but they laid no hands on the plunder" (9:16). Although the desire to strike back at enemies and to rid the world of anti-Semitism is understandable, is holy war commendable (booty was not taken)? Better is the way that the Book of Esther insists one celebrate the holiday of Purim—the date picked by Haman for the slaughter of the Jews, then hailed as a time of redemption: with "feasting and gladness [and] sending gifts of food to one another and to the poor" (9:22) and with "peace and security" (9:30).

The earliest reference to a Daniel (Dan'el) is that of a Ugaritic king who lived in the 14th century B.C.E. Ezek. 14:14 associates "Danel" with Noah and Job: three (gentile?) individuals known for wisdom. According to Ezek. 28:3, "Danel" knows secrets. Dan. 1:1 dates the story to the "third year of the reign of King Jehoiakim" or 606 B.C.E. (2 Chr. 36:5–7). Jehoiakim's son, Jehoiachin, ruled when Jerusalem was captured in 587. Nebuchadnezzar reigned from 605 to 552 B.C.E. but did not invade Judah until after 605. Such chronological problems are typical of folktales. The accounts of Daniel and the other Jewish youths taken into captivity reflect a time in which the imperial rule is ignorant and dangerous, rather than malevolent, and in which diaspora Jews live in peace, if not with a complete sense of security (contrasting Dan. 7–12, as we see in the next lecture). Consequently, the tales are most often regarded as products of the Persian (538–333 B.C.E.) or early Hellenistic (333–168 B.C.E.) periods. Dan. 2.4b–7.28 is written in Aramaic, the common language of the Near East from the Babylonian exile until the incursion of Hellenism; Dan. 1, 8–12 are in Hebrew, which had become a liturgical language in the Second Temple period.

Complicating the linguistic history are the Septuagint and Old Greek versions, which contain additions to the Daniel cycle: the Book of Susanna, the Prayer of Azariah and the Song of the Three, and Bel and the Dragon (all three appear in the Old Testament Apocrypha). Still more books in the corpus were found among documents discovered in 1948 at Qumran, the so-called "Dead Sea Scrolls." One, the Prayer of Nabonidus (4QprNab), may be an earlier version of Daniel 4. Daniel raises many questions of special concern to those Jews living under foreign rule: Should we eat non-kosher food? Should idols be worshipped? Should one cease to pray to God according to royal decree?

Joseph is sold by his brothers into Egyptian slavery; Moses is born in Egypt and compelled by God to return; Daniel is taken into Babylonian captivity; Esther is brought to court as part of a beauty pageant. The Jews find themselves in foreign courts not of their own volition, but on arriving, they make the best of their circumstances: Joseph gains charge of Egypt (Gen. 41:37–45); Moses bests Pharaoh; Esther becomes queen and Mordecai, the prime minister (Est. 8:1–2); Daniel is "made ruler" (2:48). All four cases present matters of the utmost seriousness: Joseph saves Egypt and his family from famine; Moses saves his people from death and slavery; Daniel's own life is continually threatened; and Esther saves her people from genocide. Variations in the role of God also inform these stories: Joseph receives divine aid in all that he does, and he makes explicit that his ability to interpret dreams comes from God (Gen. 40:8; 41:16). Moses receives divine aid but must be prompted. Daniel, like Joseph, succeeds in service to the ruler through his God-given ability to interpret dreams, as well as to tell the content of them before the interpretation (Dan. 2:19–23). The Book of Esther does not mention the Deity.

The additions to Esther feature highly symbolic dreams that give cosmic import to the story. As the Book of Daniel continues, the hero is no longer the interpreter of dreams but one in need of interpretation of his own visions. The changes mark a shift from folktale to apocalyptic literature, the subject of the final lecture. ■

Suggested Reading

Danna Nolan Fewell, *Circle of Sovereignty: A Story of Stories in Daniel 1–6*.

Michael Fox, *Character and Ideology in the Book of Esther*.

W. Lee Humphries, *Joseph and His Family: A Literary Study*.

James L. Kugel, *In Potiphar's House: The Interpretive Life of Biblical Texts*.

Lawrence Wills, *The Jew in the Court of the Foreign King: Ancient Jewish Court Legends* (Minneapolis, MN: Fortress Press, 1990).

Questions to Consider

1. Can one distinguish between a historical event presented in folktale style and a folktale that purports to describe a historical event?

2. What circumstances, if any, might warrant the violence described in the Book of Esther?

3. Why were Esther and Daniel the only Hebrew narratives expanded in the LXX?

4. What is the theology of Esther?

Apocalyptic Literature
(Isaiah 24–27, 56–66; Zechariah 9–14; Daniel 7–12)
Lecture 24

> Apocalyptic literature is a combination of a variety of other literatures. From the prophets it takes the idea of the concern to inculcate moral values and that God is active in history. From wisdom literature it takes speculation on the universe. It raises questions of theodicy. From novels it pulls from characters who are put in awkward, difficult, dangerous positions and then somehow they have to come to terms with their existence, often through the help of a divine mediary.

The genre "apocalyptic" (Greek: "revelation," "uncovering") takes its name from the last book of the New Testament: the Book of Revelation or the Apocalypse of St. John. Books are classified as apocalypses based on several features, not all of which appear in every apocalypse. The genre is notoriously hard to define. Apocalyptic materials sometimes are combined with other forms: the Apocalypse of Daniel is tacked onto folk tales.

What does apocalyptic writing do? It raises universal questions concerning the *Urzeit* (the time of creation) and the *Endzeit* (the end of time). It often leaves its symbols unmediated and unexplained; its audience may be familiar with the codes. It is primarily a written, not an oral, genre. It frequently offers a pessimistic view of history. Still, its determinism means that God has established a plan that includes redemption for those who now despair. Popular in apocalyptic literature is a sense of de-evolution. When things get bad enough, then God intervenes. Dualistic thought divides both mundane and supernatural realms into warring camps of good and evil. The cosmic war pits the heavenly hosts, led by the archangel Michael, against the forces of evil, led by such fallen angels as Mastema, Belial, and Satan, or the devil. On earth, the Sons of Light battle the Sons of Darkness (the Qumran War Scroll).

Daniel is an interpreter of dreams; he later becomes the visionary who needs others to interpret his dreams. In one vision, he sees the Son of Man awarded an everlasting dominion and needs an angelic explanation. Sometimes, these visions are unexplained, left to the reader's speculation. The motif of secrecy is part of the apocalyptic genre; it is like reading a mystery novel and not having all the pieces. Apocalyptic frequently gives itself a false or pseudonymous author by backdating its time of authorship.

Most scholars date Daniel's apocalyptic materials to the eve of the Maccabean revolt (2nd century B.C.E.). After Alexander's death (323), his empire was divided among his generals. To Ptolemy in Egypt went the satrapy "Across the River" (Dan. 2:41). In 198, at the Battle of Paneas, the descendants of Seleucis of Syria gain Judea. In about 168, rebellion breaks under the Seleucid Antiochus IV Epiphanes. The Temple is profaned ("abomination or desolation" or "desolating sacrilege," Dan. 8:1–14, 11:30; 1 Macc. 1:54; 2 Macc. 6:2), circumcision and Sabbath observance are forbidden, and Jerusalem becomes a Greek *polis*. The Hasmonean family (Maccabees) rout the Syrians and their supporters and replace the assimilationist families as rulers. Daniel's vision is, ultimately, one of redemption. His apocalypse is eschatological, and we still await its fulfillment.

We are at our own eschaton now that we've reached the end of the course. Given the enormous scope of the Old Testament/*Tanakh*, we are unable to cover many subjects: the court histories of David, the poetry of the Psalms and Lamentations, the development of the worship system, the canonical process, or how the texts were put together,archeological remains, such as the Moabite inscriptions to name a few. There is much in this text still to explore. Now you should have a good sense of how rich the material really is. ■

Suggested Reading

John J. Collins, *The Apocalyptic Imagination: An Introduction to Jewish Apocalyptic Literature*, 2nd ed.

Jacob Neusner, William Scott Green, and Ernest S. Frerichs (eds.), *Judaisms and Their Messiahs at the Turn of the Christian Era* (Cambridge/New York: Cambridge University Press, 1987).

J. Edward Wright, *The Early History of Heaven.*

Questions to Consider

1. What are the heirs of apocalyptic writing as a literary genre? Who are today's apocalyptic communities, and how should those who are not members regard them?

2. What motivates some modern readers to adopt radically eschatological, apocalyptic worldviews?

Timeline

Notes: All rounded numbers are approximate. All dates are B.C.E.

1800–1700 (Middle Bronze Age)	Patriarchs and matriarchs.
1700–1300	Israel in Egypt.
1300	Exodus from Egypt.
1280	Reign of Ramses II (1290–1224).
1250–1200	The "conquest."
1200–1000	Period of the Judges.
1000–922	Davidic monarchy; time of the (hypothetical) "J" writer.
922–722	The Divided Kingdom; time of the (hypothetical) "E" writer.
850	Elijah, Jezebel, and Ahab.
c. 750	Amos.
c. 740	Hosea.
724–722	Siege of Samaria.
722	Assyrian conquest of Israel; dispersal of the ten northern tribes.
715–687	Hezekiah rules the Southern Kingdom.

701	Sennacherib's unsuccessful siege of Jerusalem.
700	The first Isaiah.
640–609	Josiah.
622	Josiah finds the Book of Deuteronomy and implements the Deuteronimic Reforms.
c. 620–597	Jeremiah.
612	Nineveh (the Assyrian capital) falls to Babylon.
609	Josiah is killed and the Deuteronomic Reform ends.
597	First deportation to Babylon.
587	Nebuchadnezzar destroys Jerusalem; second deportation.
587–539/8	Ezekiel; the second Isaiah; the priestly writers edit J and E.
539/8	Edict of Cyrus.
522–486	Darius I; work on rebuilding the Temple begins.
c. 515	Haggai, Zech. 1–8.
465–424	Ezra (Ruth? Jonah?); editing of Proverbs.

423	Nehemiah.
400–300	Early versions of the Book of Esther and Dan. 1–6.
331	Battle of Issus: Alexander the Great conquers the Persian empire.
323–198	Judah under Ptolemaic rule.
198	Battle of Paneas: Seleucids gain Palestine.
175–163	Antiochus IV Epiphanes.
167	Maccabean revolt; Daniel 7–12.
165	Rededication of the Temple.

Glossary

Aaronides: Descendants of Aaron and a subset of the Levites who came to power during and after the Babylonian Exile.

A.D.: *Anno Domini*, in the year of our Lord (see **C.E.**).

Amarna letters: Cache of letters found in el-Amarna in Egypt, dating to the 15th century and testifying to the political turmoil in Palestine involving the Habiru.

Ammonites: Descendants of the son conceived by Lot and his older daughter (see **Moabites**).

Anthropomorphism: Describing the non-human (God, the divine presence, Wisdom) by means of human characteristics.

apocalyptic: From the Greek for "revelation" or "uncovering"; a type of literature, often ascribed to an ancient worthy, with a concern for heavenly secrets, substantial use of symbolism, and frequently an eschatological focus (e.g., Dan. 7–12).

apocrypha: From the Greek for "hidden," a term designating the books written by Jews during Hellenistic and Roman times (c. 200 B.C.E.–100 C.E.), included in the LXX, that became canonical for Catholic and Orthodox Christianity (see **Deutero-Canonical Texts**).

Apodictic Law: Absolute or unconditional law (as in the Decalogue); a characteristic of Israelite law but rare elsewhere in the ancient Near East (see also **Casuistic Law**).

Aramaic: A Semitic language closely related to Hebrew and Syriac (see **Peshitta**); parts of the books of Daniel and Ezra are in Aramaic.

Asherah: The Canaanite mother goddess, as well as the trees or groves dedicated to her.

Atrahasis: Hero of a Babylonian flood myth whose story is preserved on clay tablets dating to the 17th century B.C.E.

Baal: The Canaanite god of thunder and rain and, hence, of fertility; the popularity of his cult motivated both polemic from the prophets and the co-optation of his imagery by the psalmist. When not used as a proper name, the noun means "master" or "husband."

B.C.: Before Christ (see **B.C.E.**).

B.C.E.: Before the Common Era; a non-confessional expression for B.C.

Canaan: The geographical area between the Jordan River and the Mediterranean Sea; in Genesis, God promises it to Abraham and his descendants. The region was later called "Palestine."

canon: From the Greek for "reed, measuring stick, plumb line," the list of books considered inspired or official; the foundation documents of a community.

Casuistic Law: Standard ancient Near Eastern legal formulation that lists prohibitions and consequences for violation.

C.E.: Common Era; a non-confessional expression for A.D.

cherubim (sing. **cherub**): half-human, half-animal creatures, often depicted with wings, who guard the divine throne.

circumcision: The removal of the foreskin; the initiation ritual (for men) into the covenant community and the sign of the covenant.

codex (pl. **codices**): The book form as opposed to a scroll.

corvée: State-mandated forced labor.

Cosmology: A myth describing the ordered origin of the universe.

Cyrus Cylinder: Artifact from 528 B.C.E. reporting the Persian policy of repatriating exilic communities and promoting their cultic practices.

D (Deuteronomic) Source: One of the four (hypothetical) sources contributing to the composition of the Pentateuch; represented in the Book of Deuteronomy and likely composed in the late 7th century B.C.E. (See also **Deuteronomic History**.)

Dead Sea Scrolls: Manuscripts found in 1948 and subsequently on the shores of the Dead Sea (see **Qumran**), including numerous copies of biblical books; extremely helpful for text criticism.

decalogue: Literally "ten words"; a term designating the "ten commandments" (Exod. 20:1–17 [see also Exod. 34]; Deut. 5:6–21).

Deutero-Canonical Texts: The "second part" of the canon of the Old Testament; an alternative designation by Catholic and (Christian) Orthodox churches for the (Old Testament) Apocrypha. (See **Apocrypha**.)

Deutero-Isaiah: The "second Isaiah" who wrote to comfort the exiled community in Babylon (Isa. 40–55).

Deuteronomic History: The Book of Joshua through Second Kings; likely redacted in the early Second Temple period, the narrative displays the Deuteronomic view that righteousness is rewarded and evil, punished.

Deuteronomic Reform: See **Josianic Reform**.

Diaspora: Greek for "dispersion"; from the Babylonian Exile to the present, any place outside of Israel where Jews live.

Divination: Attempts to determine divine will or predict the future through omens, dreams, and the like.

Documentary Hypothesis: Also called the Graf-Wellhausen Hypothesis; the theory that four sources, J, E, D, and P, were combined to create the Pentateuch.

E (Elohist) Source: Hypothetical source marked by the use of "Elohim" for the Deity; likely composed in the Northern Kingdom c. 800.

Edomites: From the Hebrew for "red"; descendants of Esau who settled south of the Dead Sea; one of Israel's enemies.

El: Generic word for a god; sometimes used as a proper name, for example, the head of the Canaanite pantheon.

Elohim: Grammatically the plural of El; when used as a designation of the biblical God, it takes singular verbs.

Enumah Elish: "When on high"; the Babylonian creation myth that shares striking similarities to the Genesis cosmogony (Gen. 1).

Ephraim: A son of Joseph and one of the twelve tribes; a (poetic) name for the Northern Kingdom.

Eponymous Ancestor: Figure who gives his or her name to a group of descendants, e.g., Israel, Moab.

eschatology: Literally, "words concerning the end"; material describing the end of an age or of time and often involving the in-breaking of divine rule.

etiology: A story of origins.

Exegesis: From the Greek for "to lead out," critical interpretation of biblical material.

Form Criticism: Analytical approach to the structure of a pericope that seeks to determine genre, function, and *Sitz im Leben*.

Gemorah (Gemara): Section of the Talmud containing both legal and narrative materials; a commentary on the Mishnah that links it to the *Tanakh*.

***Gilgamesh* Epic**: Ancient Near Eastern epic, preserved on clay tablets from c. 1750 B.C.E., with parallels to the Garden of Eden and Flood stories.

Graf-Wellhausen Hypothesis: See **Documentary Hypothesis**.

Habiru: A group, comprised of various ethnicities, whose presence is attested in Canaan in texts from the second millennium B.C.E. (see **Amarna Letters**); this apparently wandering band may have some connection to the Hebrews.

Hannukah: Hebrew for "dedication"; festival celebrating the rededication of the Jerusalem Temple by the Maccabees after their defeat of Seleucid forces.

Hasidim: "Pious ones" who resisted the assimilationist mandates of Antiochus IV Epiphanes.

Hasmoneans: From Hasmon, the grandfather of Judah Maccabee; another name for the Macabees, usually used in reference to the dynasty they founded.

Hebrew: A Semitic language in which most of the Old Testament/*Tanakh* is written; a Semitic population group descended from Eber (an eponymous ancestor, Gen. 10:24); a designation for the covenant community from the patriarchal period until the Babylonian exile, perhaps derived from the Hebrew "to cross over."

Hellenism: Greek thought and culture brought to the East by the conquests of Alexander the Great.

Henotheism: Belief in one supreme god among many divine beings.

Hermeneutics: Term derived from the Greek god Hermes; biblical interpretation related to Exegesis but often with the connotation of involving the presuppositions and goals of the interpreter.

Hexateuch: The first six scrolls (Genesis–Joshua); a theory that the first part of Israel's story ends with the "conquering" of the Promised Land.

Hittites: Non-Semitic people, centered in the second millennium B.C.E. in Syria and Asia Minor.

Horeb: E's name for Sinai; location of Elijah's theophany.

Hyksos: Asiatic group who ruled Egypt from c. 1710 until being expelled by Pharaoh Ahmose c. 1570; sometimes associated with the stories of Joseph and the Exodus.

J (Yahwist [German: Jahweh] Source): Hypothetical source beginning with Gen. 2:4b and extending perhaps as far as 2 Sam. 7; marked by anthropomorphic descriptions of God, the use of the name YHWH before the Exodus, the reiteration of the promises of descendants, land, and blessing; usually dated to the Southern Kingdom (Judah) c. 900 B.C.E.

Jehovah: See **YHWH**.

Josianic Reform: Sponsored by King Josiah in Judah c. 622 B.C.E. and supported by the discovery of a version of what became the Book of Deuteronomy; its major action was the centralization of the cult in Jerusalem.

Judah: Son of Jacob; tribe of Israel; Southern Kingdom (following the cessation of the northern tribes under Jereboam I).

Judea: Name for and geographical location of the Post-Exilic state; attested in Ezra and Nehemiah; its inhabitants became known as "Jews."

Kenite Hypothesis: Proposal that Yahwism stems from the Kenites—perhaps through the priest of Midian, Jethro, Moses's father-in-law.

Kenites: Midianites who affiliate with Israel in the wilderness and join the settlement of Canaan.

Ketuvim: Hebrew for "writings"; the third division of the *Tanakh*.

Levites: Priestly group descended from Levi; disenfranchised from local shrines by the Josianic Reform. Following the Babylonian exile, those who are not also Aaronides become Temple workers.

LXX: Abbreviation for the Septuagint, the Greek translation of the *Tanakh*; the designation "seventy" comes from the legend that the translation was produced by seventy scribes from Jerusalem.

Maccabees: Jewish family who led the rebellion against Antiochus IV Epiphanes in 167 B.C.E.

Marduk: Patron god of Babylon and hero of the Enumah Elish.

Masoretic Text (MT): The received form of the *Tanakh*; edited and standardized by the Masoretes, Jewish scholars who added "points" (i.e., vowels), c. 7th through 9th centuries C.E.

Megillot (sing. ***Megillah***): Hebrew for "scrolls"; traditional designation for the Books of Lamentations, Ecclesiastes, Ruth, Esther, and the Song of Songs.

Merneptah Stele: Egyptian inscription erected by Pharaoh Merneptah (c. 1210) that contains the first extra-biblical reference to Israel.

messiah: Hebrew for "anointed" (Greek: Christos).

Mezuzah: Hebrew for "doorpost" and, hence, for the receptacle affixed thereon that contains passages from Deuteronomy (see Deut. 6:9).

midrash: Jewish stories that expand and/or explain biblical texts.

Mishnah: Collection of Jewish laws codified c. 200; part of the Talmud.

Moabites: Descendants of the son conceived by Lot and his younger daughter (see **Ammonites**); traditional enemies of Israel; Ruth's ethnic origin.

monotheism: Belief that there is only one God.

myth: A story of origins, often featuring divine beings, that expresses a society's self-identity.

Nazirite: An individual consecrated to God, usually for a specific period, whose practices include abstaining from wine and alcohol, avoiding corpses, and eschewing haircuts.

Nevi'im: Hebrew for "Prophets"; the second division of the *Tanakh*.

Noachide Laws: Jewish legend positing that seven laws were given to Noah to provide gentile nations with a moral code.

P (Priestly) Source: Marked by attention to law, Aaron, and genealogies, this (hypothetical) source redacted J, E, and D sometime during or soon after the Babylonian Exile.

Palestine: See **Canaan**; the name derives from the Philistines.

Pentateuch: From the Greek for "five scrolls," the first five biblical books, the Torah.

Pericope: From the Greek for "to cut around," a narrative unit that can be analyzed apart from its literary context (e.g., story, poem, saying).

Peshitta: Syriac translation of the *Tanakh* especially useful for text criticism. Syriac was a dialect of Aramaic that flourished in the early years of the common era, especially among Christians in the eastern part of the Roman empire.

Philistines: Non-Semitic, probably Mediterranean people who settled the coastal areas of Canaan in the early Iron Age (c. 1200); often enemies of Israel (Jdg.–1 Sam.) until the Davidic monarchy.

Pilgrimage Festivals: Three feasts for which it was traditional to visit the Jerusalem Temple: Passover/Feast of Unleavened bread (Hebrew, Pesach), commemorating the Exodus and the winter harvest; Weeks (Hebrew, Shavuoth; Greek, Pentecost), commemorating the giving of the Torah at Sinai fifty days later and the spring harvest; and Booths/Tabernacles (Hebrew: Sukkoth), commemorating the Exodus, the wilderness period, and the fall harvest.

Prophecy ex Eventu: Prophecy after the fact; the attribution of a text to an ancient worthy such that its description of history appears as prophecy rather than as reflection.

Prophets: The second section of the *Tanakh*.

Pseudepigrapha: Literally "false writings"; Jewish texts from Hellenistic and Roman times ascribed to ancient worthies (e.g., 4 Ezra, 2 Baruch).

Ptolemies: Heirs of Alexander the Great's general, the dynasty that governed Egypt and, from 323–198, ruled Judea.

Purim: Persian for "lots"; festival for which the etiology appears in the Book of Esther.

Qoheleth: A derivation from the Hebrew for "to assemble" (Greek: Ecclesiastes, from *Ecclesia*, "assembly"); a title for the book and the author.

Qumran: Area where the Dead Sea Scrolls were found.

Ras Shamra: Northern Syrian location where a cache of Canaanite religious texts, including Baal myths, was discovered in 1929.

redaction criticism: An analysis of concerns of the editor (redactor) of a text as determined by editorial expansion, arrangement, and comment.

Royal Grant: Covenant granted by a suzerain, sometimes as a reward for past service, and in guarantee of future aid and protection; this covenantal formulation, as opposed to the **suzerainty/vassal model**, is associated with Noah, Abraham, and especially David (2 Sam. 7; Pss. 89, 132).

Samaria: Capital of the Northern Kingdom.

Samaritans: The population of the former Northern Kingdom of Israel following the deportation by Assyria of many Israelites and the resettling in Samaria of peoples from elsewhere in the Assyrian empire.

Second Isaiah: See **Deutero-Isaiah**.

Second Temple Period: Judaism from the beginning of Persian rule to the destruction of the Temple by Rome in 70 C.E.

Seleucids: Heirs of Alexander the Great's general, the dynasty that governed Syria and, in 198, obtained Judea from the Ptolemies.

Septuagint: See **LXX**.

Shekinah: The feminine presence of the Divine.

Sheol: The home of the dead, a shadowy place below the earth; early references display no conception of punishment or reward.

Sh'ma (***Shema***): From the Hebrew for the imperative "Hear!"; the Jewish statement of faith beginning with Deut. 6:4–9.

Sinai: Today called Jebel Musa, the "Mountain of Moses"; J's expression for the traditional site of the giving of the Torah to Moses.

Sitz im Leben: German for "setting in life"; the cultural and historical context of a book or pericope.

Son of Man: A human being (Ezek., Pss.); in Dan. 7:13, the symbol of the covenant community who appears in the heavenly throne room and who is given earthly rule.

Sons of the Prophets: Bands or guilds of prophets, sometimes traveling with a prophetic leader, such as Elijah or Elisha.

Sophia: Greek for "Wisdom"; the personification of Wisdom in female form.

stele: A free-standing pillar with inscriptions.

Suzerainty/Vassal Treaty: Covenant formulation between unequal parties guaranteeing protection on the part of the suzerain and fidelity on the part of the vassal; the form of the Mosaic covenant (see **Royal Grant**).

tabernacle: The wilderness shrine that housed the Ark (see Exod. 25–40).

Talmud: A compendium of Jewish law and lore consisting of the Mishnah and the Gemorah; the Babylonian Talmud was codified c. 700 C.E. and the Palestinian, c. 400 C.E.

Tanakh **(*Tanak, Tanach*)**: Acronym for "*Torah, Nevi'im, Ketuvim*"; a way of designating the canon used by the synagogue.

targum: An Aramaic translation/paraphrase of a biblical book.

tefillin (Greek: *phylacteries*): Small boxes containing scriptural passages that are worn on the left hand and forehead for worship and kept in place by straps wrapped, respectively, seven times around the left arm and around the head.

tel (***tell***): From the Hebrew/Arabic for "hill," an artificial mound created by the layers of habitation debris.

Tetragrammaton: Expression for the "four letters" (consonants) that stand for the personal name of the Deity (see **YHWH**).

text (textual) criticism (low criticism): Method for determining the original wording of a text.

theodicy: From the Greek for "justice of god," the question of why the wicked prosper and the righteous suffer.

theophany: From the Greek for "god's appearance," a manifestation of the Divine.

Torah: Hebrew for "instruction" or "law"; the first five books of the Bible.

Twelve, Book of the: The collection also known as the "Minor Prophets": Hosea, Joel, Amos, Obadiah, Jonah, Micah, Nahum, Habakkuk, Zephaniah, Haggai, Zechariah, and Malachi.

type scene: A literary convention; manipulation of the conventional elements entertainingly reveals character development; examples include the "ancestress in danger," the "woman at the well," "annunciations," and "rival wives."

Ugarit: Canaanite city in modern Syria; location of a major cache of Canaanite myths.

vulgate: From the Latin for "common," St. Jerome's translation of the Hebrew canon into Latin in 405 C.E.

Wisdom Literature: An international genre addressing questions of theodicy and nature and how to live the good life. Biblical examples are Proverbs, Ecclesiastes (Qoheleth), and Job; the Old Testament Apocrypha/Deuterocanonical collection offers Wisdom of Solomon and the Wisdom of Jesus Ben Sirach (Sirach, Ecclesiasticus).

YHWH: The personal name of God, likely meaning "he will be what he will be"; it is not pronounced in Jewish liturgical settings. English translations usually render this term as "Lord" (the four letters in each facilitate remembering the connection).

Ziggurat (Ziqqurat): Mesopotamian temple in the form of a terraced mountain or pyramid erected to serve as a symbolic bridge between heaven and earth.

Zion: Another name for Jerusalem; the Temple mount.

Bibliography

Essential Reading: The Old Testament/the *Tanakh*.

Note: The Hebrew is to be preferred in all cases. No translation can capture the riches of the original: the puns, the polyvalency, and ambiguity. Should the reader not be fluent in biblical Hebrew (which is not the same as modern Hebrew), several very good translations are available. These include, but are not limited to, the ones listed below.

Everett Fox, *The Five Books of Moses: Genesis, Exodus, Leviticus, Numbers, Deuteronomy: A New Translation with Introductions, Commentary, and Notes* (New York, Schocken Books, 1995): An attempt to preserve the sense of the Hebrew (better when read aloud). See also Fox's *Give us a King! Samuel, Saul, and David: A New Translation of Samuel I and II* (New York: Schocken Books, 1999).

The Jewish Publication Society (JPS) version: *Tanakh: A New Translation of the Holy Scripture According to the Traditional Hebrew Text*.

The King James Version (KJV) or "Authorized Version" is the one with language most familiar to English speakers. The volume was commissioned by King James I of England for use in the Anglican Church. It is, however, often difficult to understand, and its renditions of the Hebrew do not have the advantage of more recent manuscript discoveries, linguistic study, or the witness of the Dead Sea Scrolls. It also occasionally adapts the Hebrew to the Christological concerns of the New Testament.

The New American Bible (NAB): Translation produced by and for Roman Catholics.

The New International Version (NIV): Produced by and for Protestant Evangelicals.

The New Revised Standard Version (NRSV): Substantially the same as the RSV, but gender inclusive (which sometimes skews the connotations of the Hebrew). Several editions with critical notes from interfaith scholarly contributors are available, for example, Gail R. O'Day and David Petersen (gen. eds.), *The Access Bible: New Revised Standard Version, with the Apocryphal/Deuterocanonical Books* (New York: Oxford University Press, 1999).

The Revised Standard Version (RSV): An essentially literal translation but with updated language.

I encourage students to avoid modern paraphrases, such as *Good News for Modern Man* and *Today's English Version* (TEV).

Note: Studies of the Old Testament/*Tanakh* have been produced since the Hellenistic period; written by Jews, Christians, and Unitarians, as well as atheists, agnostics, and members of other traditions; they are found in synagogues and churches, seminary libraries and secular bookstores, in private homes and in museums. The bibliographic items listed after each chapter and below offer only a small representation of the academic study of the Bible. I have attempted to avoid works requiring knowledge of ancient languages, works requiring a nearby divinity school or seminary library (including articles in professional journals), and works with a relatively narrow denominational or confessional focus. I have attempted to include works that present a variety of opinions and approaches and to list primarily recent studies (in almost all cases, the sources listed below have their own bibliographical references to earlier scholarship). I also list several encyclopedias and dictionaries.

Resources:

Achtemeier, Paul J. (gen. ed.), *The HarperCollins Bible Dictionary* (San Francisco: Harper San Francisco, 1996): Dictionary produced in cooperation with the Society of Biblical Literature (a major professional society of biblical scholars).

Aharoni, Yohanan, and Michael Avi-Yonah, *The Macmillan Bible Atlas* (New York: Macmillan, 1977).

Brown, Raymond, Joseph A. Fitzmyer, and Roland E. Murphy (eds.), *The New Jerome Biblical Commentary* (Englewood Cliffs, NJ: Prentice Hall, 1999).

Coogan, Michael D. (ed.), *The Oxford History of the Biblical World* (New York: Oxford University Press, 1998): Articles by leading scholars on the historical and cultural periods in which biblical events took shape.

Farmer, William R. (ed.), *The International Bible Commentary: A Catholic and Ecumenical Commentary for the Twenty-First Century* (Collegeville, MN: Liturgical Press, 1998).

Freedman, D. N., et al., *The Anchor Bible Dictionary*, six vols. (New York: Doubleday, 1992; available on CD-ROM): Signed articles by leading scholars; inclusive bibliographies; a major resource for scholar and lay reader alike.

Hayes, John H. (gen. ed.), *Dictionary of Biblical Interpretation*, 2 vols. (Nashville: Abingdon, 1999): Major scholars and methods.

Knight, Douglas A., and Gene M. Tucker (eds.), *The Hebrew Bible and Its Modern Interpreters* (Philadelphia: Fortress Press, 1985): Excellent collection of essays on the major issues and theories in academic biblical study.

Matthews, Victor H., and Don C. Benjamin, *Old Testament Parallels: Laws and Stories from the Ancient Near East* (New York: Paulist Press, 1991).

Metzger, Bruce M., and Michael D. Coogan (eds.), *The Oxford Companion to the Bible* (New York: Oxford University Press, 1993): Short articles on major figures, events, locations, and other topics in dictionary format.

Newsom, Carol A., and Sharon H. Ringe (eds.), *The Women's Bible Commentary* (Louisville: Westminster/John Knox, 1992): Essays by women academics that combine more traditional approaches with attention to gender roles, women's history, and hermeneutical implications.

Shanks, Herschel (ed.), *Bible Review* (as well its sister publication, *Biblical Archaeology Review*): An often original, sometimes irreverent magazine written by scholars but designed for the general public; the illustrations are superb.

Series (commentaries on individual books, as well as major subject areas):

Anchor Bible (New York: Doubleday).

Anchor Bible Reference Library (New York: Doubleday).

Berit Olam (Collegeville, MN: Liturgical Press).

Feminist Companions, edited by Athalya Brenner (Sheffield: University Press).

Hermeneia (Philadelphia: Fortress Press).

New Interpreter's Bible (Nashville: Abingdon).

The Old Testament Library (Louisville: Westminster/John Knox).

Introductions (a few among many):

Anderson, Bernard, *Understanding the Old Testament*, 4th ed. (Englewood Cliffs: Prentice Hall, 1986).

Flanders, Henry Jackson, Jr., Robert Wilson Crapps, and David Anthony Smith, *People of the Covenant: An Introduction to the Hebrew Bible*, 4th ed. (New York: Oxford University Press, 1996).

Frick, Frank S., *A Journey through the Hebrew Scriptures* (Fort Worth: Harcourt Brace College Publishers, 1995).

Gottwald, Norman K., *The Hebrew Bible: A Socio-Literary Introduction* (Philadelphia: Fortress Press, 1985).

Levenson, Jon D., *Sinai and Zion: An Entry into the Jewish Bible* (Minneapolis: Winston, 1985).

Individual Studies:

Ackerman, Susan, *Warrior, Dancer, Seductress, Queen: Women in Judges and Biblical Israel*, Anchor Bible Reference Library (New York: Doubleday, 1998).

Alter, Robert, *The Art of Biblical Narrative* (New York: Basic Books, 1981): A prize-winning literary critical study that popularized the study of type scenes, traced the impact of themes and even key words throughout different books, and explored the importance of the juxtaposition of stories for mutual interpretation.

Anderson, Gary, Michael Stone, and Johannes Tromp (eds.), *Literature on Adam and Eve: Collected Essays*, Studies in Veteris Testamenti Pseudepigrapa (Leiden and Boston: E. J. Brill, 2000).

Bailey, Lloyd R., *Noah: The Person and the Story in History and Tradition* (Columbia, SC: University of South Carolina Press, 1989).

Bal, Mieke, *Death and Dissymmetry: The Politics of Coherence in the Book of Judges* (Chicago: University of Chicago Press, 1988).

Ballentine, Samuel E., *Prayer in the Hebrew Bible* (Philadelphia: Fortress, 1993).

———, *The Torah's Vision of Worship* (Minneapolis: Fortress, 1999).

Barr, James, *The Garden of Eden and the Hope of Immortality* (Philadelphia: Fortress, 1993).

Blenkinsopp, Joseph, *The Pentateuch: An Introduction to the First Five Books of the Bible*, Anchor Bible Reference Library (New York: Doubleday, 1992): A good overview of approaches, with a helpful description of the Documentary Hypothesis.

Brueggemann, Walter, *Theology of the Old Testament: Testimony, Dispute, Advocacy* (Minneapolis: Fortress Press, 1997).

Collins, John J., *The Apocalyptic Imagination: An Introduction to Jewish Apocalyptic Literature*, 2nd ed. (Grand Rapids, MI: William B. Eerdmans, 1998).

Craig, Kenneth M., *The Poetics of Jonah: Art in the Service of Ideology*, 2nd ed. (Macon, GA: Mercer University Press, 1999).

Delaney, Carol Lowery, *Abraham on Trial: The Social Legacy of Biblical Myth* (Princeton, NJ: Princeton University Press, 1998).

Dever, William G., *Recent Archaeological Discoveries and Biblical Research* (Seattle: University of Washington Press, 1990).

Douglas, Mary, *Purity and Danger: An Analysis of Concepts of Pollution and Taboo* (London/Boston: Ark Paperbacks, 1966, 1984).

Dundes, Alan (ed.), *The Flood Myth* (Berkeley: University of California Press, 1988).

———, *Holy Writ as Oral Lit: The Bible as Folklore* (Lanham, MD: Rowan and Littlefield, 1999).

Eilberg-Schwartz, Howard, *The Savage in Judaism: An Anthropology of Israelite Religion and Judaism* (Bloomington: Indiana University Press,

1990): Prize-winning, controversial study of ritual practice and the use of metaphor.

Exum, J. Cheryl, *Fragmented Women: Feminist Subversions of Biblical Narratives* (Sheffield: JSOT Press, 1993).

Falk, Marcia, *Love Lyrics from the Bible, The Song of Sons: A New Translation and Interpretation* (San Francisco: HarperCollins, 1990): Poet and linguist happily meet.

Fewell, Danna Nolan, *Circle of Sovereignty: A Story of Stories in Daniel 1–6* (Sheffield: Almond Press, 1988).

Fox, Michael, *Character and Ideology in the Book of Esther* (Columbia, SC: University of South Carolina Press, 1991).

Friedman, Richard Elliott, *Who Wrote the Bible?* (Englewood Cliffs: Prentice-Hall, 1987). Idiosyncratic but extremely engaging study.

Harrelson, Walter, *The Ten Commandments and Human Rights* (Philadelphia: Fortress Press, 1981): A study by a leading Old Testament scholar of how the Bible has been, and can be, used for purposes of social justice.

Humphries, W. Lee, *Joseph and his Family: A Literary Study* (Columbia, SC: University of South Carolina Press, 1988).

Jobling, David, *First Samuel* (Collegeville, MN: Liturgical Press, 1998).

Kirsch, Jonathan, *Moses: A Life* (New York: Bantam Books, 1998).

Kugel, James L., *In Potiphar's House: The Interpretive Life of Biblical Texts* (San Francisco: HarperCollins, 1990).

———, *Traditions of the Bible: A Guide to the Bible as It Was at the Start of the Common Era* (Cambridge, MA: Harvard University Press, 1998).

Kvam, Kristen, Linda S. Schearing, and Valarie H. Ziegler, *Eve and Adam: Jewish, Christian and Muslim Readings on Genesis and Gender* (Bloomington: Indiana University Press, 1999).

Larsson, Göran, *Bound for Freedom: The Book of Exodus in Jewish and Christian Traditions* (Peabody, MA: Hendrikson, 1999).

Lemche, Niels Peter, *Early Israel: Anthropological and Historical Studies on the Israelite Society before the Monarchy* (Leiden: E.J. Brill, 1985).

Levenson, Jon D., *Death and Resurrection of the Beloved Son: The Transformation of Child Sacrifice in Judaism and Christianity* (New Haven: Yale University Press, 1993).

Matthews, Victor H., Bernard Levinson, and Tikva Frymer-Kensky, *Gender and Law in the Hebrew Bible and the Ancient Near East* (Sheffield: Sheffield Academic Press, 1998).

Mazar, Amihai, *Archaeology of the Land of the Bible: 10,000–586 B.C.E.* (New York: Bantam Doubleday Dell, 1990).

McKenzie, Stephen L., *King David: A Biography* (Oxford and New York: Oxford University Press, 2000).

Meyers, Carol, *Discovering Eve: Ancient Israelite Women in Context* (New York: Oxford University Press, 1988): Prize-winning, innovative study combining sociology, archaeology, and linguistics.

Murphy, Roland E., *The Tree of Life: An Exploration of Biblical Wisdom Literature* (New York: Doubleday, 1990).

Neusner, Jacob, William Scott Green, and Ernest S. Frerichs (eds.), *Judaisms and Their Messiahs at the Turn of the Christian Era* (Cambridge/New York: Cambridge University Press, 1987).

Niditch, Susan, *Ancient Israelite Religion* (New York: Oxford University Press, 1997).

———, *Folklore and the Hebrew Bible* (Philadelphia: Fortress Press, 1993).

———, *War in the Hebrew Bible: A Study in the Ethics of Violence* (New York: Oxford University Press, 1997).

Olyan, Saul, *Rites and Rank: Hierarchy in Biblical Representations of Cult* (Princeton, NJ: Princeton University Press, 2000.

Perdue, Leo, and Clark Gilpin (eds.), *The Voice from the Whirlwind: Interpreting the Book of Job* (Nashville: Abingdon, 1992): Studies addressing historical, literary, and theological issues edited by a professor of biblical studies and a theologian.

Rendtorff, Rolf, *The Covenant Formula: An Exegetical and Theological Investigation*, Margaret Kohl, trans. (Edinburgh: T&T Clark, 1998).

Rogerson, John, and Philip Davies, *The Old Testament World* (Englewood Cliffs, NJ: Prentice-Hall, 1989).

Sawyer, John F. A. (ed.), *Reading Leviticus: A Conversation with Mary Douglas* (Sheffield: Sheffield Academic Press, 1996).

Smith, Mark, *The Early History of God: Yahweh and Other Deities in Ancient Israel* (San Francisco: Harper, 1990).

Spiegel, Shalom, *The Last Trial*, Judah Golden, trans. (New York: Schocken, 1969): Fascinating study of the history of the interpretation of the *Akedah* (Gen. 22).

Steussy, Marti J., *David: Biblical Portraits of Power* (Columbia, SC: University of South Carolina Press, 1999).

Trible, Phyllis, *Texts of Terror: Literary-Feminist Readings of Biblical Narratives* (Philadelphia: Fortress Press, 1984).

Wills, Lawrence, *The Jew in the Court of the Foreign King: Ancient Jewish Court Legends* (Minneapolis, MN: Fortress Press, 1990).

Wright, J. Edward, *The Early History of Heaven* (New York: Oxford University Press, 2000).

Yee, Gail (ed.), *Judges and Method: New Approaches in Biblical Studies* (Minneapolis: Fortress Press, 1995).

Notes

Notes